D1370486

STONE BUILT

STONE BUILT

CONTEMPORARY AMERICAN HOUSES

LEE GOFF

INTRODUCTION BY CHARLES GWATHMEY

THE MONACELLI PRESS

First published in the United States of
America in 1997 by
The Monacelli Press, Inc.
10 East 92nd Street, New York, New York 10128.

Copyright © 1997 The Monacelli Press, Inc.,
and Lee Goff

All rights reserved under International and Pan-
American Copyright Conventions. No part of this
book may be reproduced or utilized in any form or
by any means, electronic or mechanical, including
photocopying, recording, or by any information
storage and retrieval system, without permission in
writing from the publisher. Inquiries should be sent
to The Monacelli Press, Inc.

Library of Congress Cataloging-in-Publication Data
Goff, Lee.
Stone built : contemporary American houses /
Lee Goff ; introduction by Charles Gwathmey.
p. cm.
Includes bibliographical references.
ISBN 1-885254-69-5
1. Stone houses—United States—Pictorial works.
2. Architecture, Modern—20th century—United
States—Pictorial works. I. Title.
NA7210.G64   1997
721'.0441'0973—dc21   97-28730

Printed and bound in Italy

Designed by Abigail Sturges

Half-title page: Marlys Hahn, Mountain Retreat
Title pages: Deamer + Phillips, Rich Residence

Photography Credits
Arch Image: 252–53, 255, 256, 257, 258–59
Assassi Productions: 13, 14, 15, 16–17
Karl A. Backus: 207, 208–9, 211, 212, 213, 214, 215,
216–17, 218–19, 220, 221, 222–23, 224, 225, 226–27
Lisa Carol & Paul Hester Photographers: 127, 128, 129,
130, 131
Cobblestone Society: 26
Paul Ferrino: 172–73, 175, 176, 177, 178, 179, 180, 181
Oberto Gili: 92–93, 95, 96, 97, 98–99
Anton Grassl: 2–3, 106–7, 108, 109, 110–11, 112, 113,
114–15
HABS, courtesy of Cliveden of the National Trust, Inc.:
23 top
John M. Hall: 142–43, 144, 145, 146, 147, 148–49
Henry Whitfield Historical Museum, Connecticut Historical
Commission: 22 top
Paul Hester Photographer: 124–25
Paul Hester & Lisa Hardaway Photographers: 58–59, 61, 62,
63, 64–65, 66–67
Greg Hursley: 68–69, 70, 71, 72, 73, 74–75, 76, 77, 78, 79,
80–81, 83, 86, 88, 89
Timothy Hursley: 151, 162–63, 164–65, 166, 167, 168, 169,
170, 171
Ron Johnson: 236–37, 239, 240–41
Tom Kessler: 46–47, 48–49, 50, 51, 52–53, 54, 55, 56–57
Robert C. Lautman: 91, 116–17, 118, 119, 120, 121, 122,
123
Hans Lettner: 100–101, 103, 104, 105, 228–29, 230, 231,
232–33, 234–35
Library of Congress, Prints and Photographs Division, HABS:
21 (VA-256), 22 bottom , 25 bottom (NY-5538A-6)
Christopher Little: 82, 84, 85, 87
Ron Livieri: 260–61, 262, 263, 264, 265, 266, 267, 268–69
James C. Massey: 23 bottom, 25 top, 27 bottom
Ben Mitchell: 1, 242–43, 244, 247
Old House Journal: 24, 28 bottom
Paul Rocheleau: 23 center, 27 top, 28 top
Michael Scott: 192–93, 194, 195, 196, 197
Taft Architects: 198–99, 201, 202, 203, 204, 205
Bruce van Inwegen: 182–83, 184, 185, 186, 187, 188–89,
190–91
Paul Warchol: 34, 35, 37, 38, 39, 132–33, 134, 135, 136,
137, 138–39, 140–41, 245, 246, 248, 249, 250, 251
Matt Wargo: 33, 40, 41, 42, 43, 44–45
Christopher Wesnofske: 152–53, 154, 155, 156–57, 159,
160–61

CONTENTS

ACKNOWLEDGMENTS

I want to thank Cynthia Conigliaro, my former classmate and now an owner of the Manhattan bookstore Archivia. She suggested the topic and contributed her encouragement and friendship along with many helpful suggestions. I wish to express appreciation to my publisher, Gianfranco Monacelli; to my editor, Andrea Monfried, whose expertise guided me through the twists and turns of the book's publication; and to Abigail Sturges, whose design created an elegant book that so well expresses the subject. Professor Martin Weaver of Columbia University's Graduate School of Architecture, Planning and Preservation gave me early encouragement, for which I am grateful. I also thank Lorenzo Semple, who read an early draft and offered valuable comments, and Ronald Konicky, who provided the benefit of his expert legal advice.

Special thanks goes to those who kindly supplied information and photographs of historic houses: Elizabeth Laurent, Cliveden Museum; Delia Robinson, Cobblestone Resource Center; Michael McBride, Henry Whitfield State Museum; Timothy Harley, Huguenot Historical Society; and Susan Brillantes, *Old House Journal*. My gratitude also goes to the superb photographer Paul Rocheleau for contributing his excellent images to the history section.

I am indebted to the architects represented and to their staffs for their cooperation and generosity in supplying the necessary materials. Finally, I am particularly grateful to Charles Gwathmey for his words of introduction and his design of a stone house. Without his work, no book on contemporary houses would be complete.

FOR BILL

FOR BILL

Read the grammar of the Earth in a particle of stone!
Stone is the frame on which his Earth is modeled,
and wherever it crops out—there the architect may
sit and learn.

—FRANK LLOYD WRIGHT, *In the Cause of Architecture*

PREFACE

We live in a world surrounded by the synthetic, the temporary, the disposable, a world of momentariness in which permanence, because it is disappearing, is all the more captivating. When I began research for this book, I found that mention of stone houses prompted enthusiastic responses from almost everyone. People wanted me to know about vernacular dwellings in all regions, from the cobblestone residences in upstate New York to the German rock houses in Fredericksburg, Texas. We take special notice of stone houses, remember and value them, not only because they are exceptional in a country where most houses are made of wood, but because of what they say to us about timelessness and permanence. In addition, stone gives texture, detail, and dimension to a structure in a way that no other material does. Whether vernacular or contemporary, stone's charisma is its ability to evoke an emotional response, an appeal to the desire to touch.

Stone is being employed increasingly as a major medium in domestic designs. The architects represented in this book all praised it as a building material. William Leddy summed up: "Architects love stone. It connects building and place, man and nature. It is timeless, primal. It creates powerful, positive associations about home and hearth. Stone connects to the making of the building, the human hand, and the people who made it."

Clients choose stone for a variety of reasons. It is labor intensive and ever the status material, and a serious stone house continues to be a means of celebrating success. But more than implications of wealth, the underlying appeal is solidity and durability. Juergen Riehm, of the firm 1100 Architect, feels that for many people it conveys something beyond mere show: "They want something that is not just thrown together. More people are recognizing that stone has a greater value; it's a very different appearance." Indeed, many architects told me that the increasing demand for stone houses is a reaction to construction's version of fifteen-minute-fame—flashy but flimsy building. In addition, architects have found more economical paths to employing stone, making its use possible in a greater variety of projects. As some of the houses in this book demonstrate, they are using recycled curbing stones, stone tailings, and stone excavated from the site, as well as creative design that reduces the amount of stone required. Whether a house is sixteen rooms or six, building stone is in increasing demand.

The historic preservation movement of the mid-1960s brought about a renewed concern with local materials and the environment. Postmodernism freed design from the strictures of modernism and led to great diversity in design. Both movements engendered an interest in natural materials such as stone. The houses in this book represent a range of styles, from classical and traditional to abstract modernism. Whatever the design expression, some common themes emerge.

Stone is used to relate the structure to its setting, as anchor to the ground, whether in foundations, chimneys, a wall, or the entire house. "Stone is so much a part of the geology of place," says Will Bruder, who never imports stone. Like Frank Lloyd Wright, he uses it inside his Arizona desert houses, as well as out, to merge interiors with the natural landscape.

Vernacular precedents are another recurring theme. Even the most modernist houses, such as Deamer + Phillips's Massachusetts residence, reflect historic regional references, uniting past and present. In the case of Deamer + Phillips, the associations are translated through a modernist vision that reinterprets them in an innovative way, placing the house firmly in the late twentieth century.

The contemporary palette of building materials includes wood, glass, steel, and concrete, as well as stone. Peter Forbes believes that it is the role of the architect to edit among materials to give each its own value. Frequently in the houses represented here, stone contrasts its monumental solidity with the weightless transparency of glass or its stony roughness with the satin smoothness of wood. In houses with great expanses of glass, stone is used to enclose interior spaces, providing a refuge that satisfies the human desire for an inner sanctum, a cave.

The unique nature of stone's strength is expressed through compression. When units of stone are stacked upon each other, they are in compression. In the mid-nineteenth century, with the introduction of steel and the need for insulation, stone ceased to be used as a structural material; its function became one of cladding. In fact, only a few of the houses illustrated here have solid stone walls. However, none of the architects apply stone in the manner of thin veneer. All stonework is thick enough to create a substantial mass. In many cases, the stones are stacked on each other and the foundation of the house is extended beyond its wood frame to carry their weight.

In each period, the names of architectural titans have been attached to important houses of stone—Richard Morris Hunt; McKim, Mead & White; H. H. Richardson; Frank Lloyd Wright; Greene & Greene. So, too, today. The houses presented here were chosen to show how contemporary architects of the first rank are using stone as a primary material in domestic designs.

Shakespeare wrote: "And this our life, exempt from public haunt, / Finds Tongues in trees, books in the running brooks, / Sermons in stones, and good in everything." The naturalist John Burroughs saw it differently: "Nature teaches more than she preaches. There are no sermons in stones. It is easier to get a spark out of a stone than a moral." Perhaps not a moral but surely a murmured message of time and age, of builder, humankind, and landscape. Whether rustic cabin or crenelated castle, stone houses continue to draw us with their romantic appeal.

INTRODUCTION

CHARLES GWATHMEY

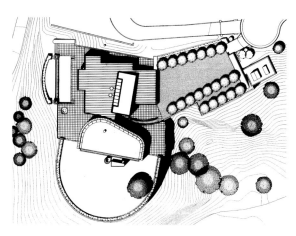

OPPOSITE: *The pool terrace faces west; at the end is a glimpse of the limestone wall that defines the southern portion of the house. The two-level site embodies the majesty, quiet, and timelessness of Malibu Canyon, in contrast to the sparkling, sun-drenched horizon of the day and the equally sparkling city lights of the night.*

Stonehenge, the Great Wall of China, the Pyramids, Roman aqueducts, Carcassonne: stone embodies permanence, density, and eternalness. Equally, stone implies legitimacy, integrity, and stability. In recent contemporary architecture, stone has reemerged as an enclosure material—as opposed to a planar material—and this book confirms that reality. Stone has become a primary material in my own recent work as well, which is why I agreed to write this introduction.

I have enjoyed evaluating these houses through the eyes of an unapologetically modern architect. I noted historicist and traditional manifestations as well as investigations into abstraction. The work has been enriched by the use of stone: formally, hierarchically, and materially. While I may be unsympathetic to some of the stylistic approaches, since intellectually I do not believe in replication, it is interesting to see the many ways stone has been represented, each house exploring the possibilities and the implications of the material on its own terms.

The use of stone is a serious commitment, since it is connotatively loaded. It is possible to fall into the trap of credibility, that is, that stone for stone's sake is automatically positive. If stone is truly to be considered a material for our time, architects must examine the possibilities in terms of invention, transformation, and abstraction, not replication or representation. In other words, stone is no guarantee; it is either an added burden or an opportunity. If the designer accepts the investigative and interrogative process of discovery, he or she can change the status quo, and create a work that is confrontational, provocative, and subversive—the idea and the obligation of art.

I come to this introduction not only with my own point of view, but with my own stone house. As I discussed this book with Lee Goff, I realized that I could present this new house as a case study from the perspective of the architect, rather than the critic, which is a rare opportunity.

We chose to use stone in our Pacific Palisades house in response to a unique site that offered an opportunity to establish counterpoint and the unexpected contradiction. The investigation consistently and rigorously explores the idea of duality. The site, a small, two-level plateau on the side of the Palisades, visually intersects the Los Angeles Valley, the California coast, the Pacific Ocean, and the initiation of Malibu Canyon. This juxtaposition afforded an opportunity to design two distinctly different ideals and combine them into a cubist architectural collage.

A limestone wall, conceptually an excavated fragment or ruin, is perched as an object on the plateau with its open side facing south. A pavilion is then hung within the stone object, establishing a dialogue of intervention and counterpoint. The juxtaposition of materials—stone and stucco, steel and glass—engages primary perceptions: gravity and weightlessness, natural and human-made, realized and implied, fragment and whole, enclosure and openness, solid and void, volume and plane.

The pavilion itself engages the landscape and becomes a volume carved into the canyon. It is both the equal and the opposite of the limestone wall. While the stone wall sits on the land, the pavilion and its extension sit within the stone form and the natural topography. The object on the land and the object in the land counterbalance and exploit the multidimensional site. This would have been impossible without stone, both as a material brought to the project and as a material inherent in the project. It is conceptual and real, present and past, found and made.

This house may serve as a counterpoint to the other houses in this book as well as a point of departure. In the end we (architects) are all interested in stone: the multiplicities, the possibilities, the unequaled qualities inherent in the material.

ABOVE AND RIGHT: *The main entry to the house is on the upper level from the driveway; another entrance is on the lower level along the limestone wall, which is thirty-two feet high and two-and-one-half feet thick.*

OPPOSITE: *The curvilinear limestone wall defines the living room.*

OVERLEAF: *A facade of glass is held in tension along the open, south side of the limestone wall. The pavilion interrupting the glass floats both within and without the "found ruin" of the wall.*

A BRIEF HISTORY
OF STONE HOUSES
IN AMERICAN
ARCHITECTURE

Stone. The very word evokes an image of power, of absolute strength, impregnability, endurance. Even more subliminally, it conveys a sense of the primordial; we instinctively feel the millions of years it took to form. Rock is the fundamental building material of this planet's crust and the original material used by humans for shelter from the elements. From Asia to Africa, neolithic peoples gathered fieldstones to build the first basic houses. When shaped to human needs, natural rock is called stone. Primitive people and advanced cultures alike have fashioned stone not only to create shelter, but also to fulfill the need for artistic expression.[1]

With simple tools ancient civilizations carved and corbeled hewn blocks of stone, sculpted, squared, and stacked them, and exposed their colors to express a beauty possible only with stone. Today people flock to such places as Ephesus, Petra, and Angkor Wat to wonder at the achievement of the civilizations that built them and to sense the connection with the past that is provided by anything so enduring. I experienced awe and fascination on a visit to Tikal one wet afternoon. From the steep height of a Mayan temple, I gazed out at other towering pyramids eerily shrouded in gray mist above the lush canopy of the Yucatan jungle. I marveled at what had been achieved with hand-wrought tools and elemental material. For an instant, I envisioned the plaza below alive with people. But the civilization had disappeared centuries ago, and the unrelenting jungle, once beaten back by the Indians, had captured the abandoned city. It remained so until this century when human forces drove back the tropical vegetation once more to reveal the temples, palaces, and plazas in all their beauty and in an endurance that defied the powerful forces of time and nature.

In the United States we are drawn to such ancient stonework as the Native American cliff dwellings at Mesa Verde and Canyon de Chelly, rock shelters carved into daunting cliffs between A.D. 350 and 1300. Compelling, too, are the red sandstone formations that rise from the floor of our great western deserts, nature's own architecture of pinnacles, spires, and arches designed by the sculpting forces of wind and water.

While North America is known as a land of timber, a unique and highly diverse history of domestic architecture in stone also exists. Such houses make up only a small percentage of dwellings, but they include a great variety of styles, techniques, and types of stone. Indeed, in the story of American architecture, from the earliest folk houses to contemporary formal architectural designs, stone houses form a chapter of their own. The regional vernacular house types that various groups built as they settled the Atlantic seaboard and then began moving into the vast territory between the Appalachian Mountains and the Mississippi River and beyond demonstrate practical solutions that have become a source of inspiration for many architects in the postmodern era. Many of the early stone houses have endured not only to outlast fashionable styles but also to tell the story of the immigrants who built them. Those who used stone transformed an element of landscape into a material of shelter, and the forms the houses took were themselves a reflection of the stone.

Each building material speaks its own language. Frank Lloyd Wright wrote that wood communicates "grain and silken surface" (or should be allowed to).[2] But if wood speaks one tongue, stone is multilingual. A mosaic wall of stone conveys texture, color, pattern, scale, and skill that cannot be found in any other material. It also speaks an abstract language of metaphor and symbol. Houses clad in wood have special qualities of lightness, form, and uniquely suited styles, but they do not conjure up an image of the forest primeval, especially when, as Wright said, "encased in an armor of paint." A fieldstone house, however, calls to mind the ledges of a quarry or the millennia-old rocky outcroppings in the landscape. The rock's rough gray edges speak to the earth they came from, conveying a link to the most permanent world of all—the natural world.

Stone has its own set of terms as a medium of construction. Used in its natural state, left unworked from the quarry or collected from fields and shorelines and retaining a natural outline, it is referred to as *rubble*. *Random rubble* refers to fieldstones in various sizes and shapes laid rather like a jigsaw puzzle, with relatively thick mortar joints. *Coursed random rubble* refers to rough-faced stones laid horizontally as they are found in nature, bedded in strata. The effect of rubble stonework is informal, picturesque, and romantic. When stone is squared and sawn so that its exposed surfaces take on a quality of bricklike uniformity, sometimes honed or polished to reveal attractive patterns, it is called *ashlar*. The squared effect is formal, carrying associations of the solidity of public buildings and the affluence of banks and formal houses. The term *masonry* originally applied only to stonework but has come to include brick and concrete. In this book, it is used in that original sense, applying only to stonework.

Until about 1840, houses were built with solid walls of a thickness adequate to support their height, often two feet or more. The decorative facade stones were backed by smaller, less refined stones. Large tie-stones were used to bond the whole together to prevent the wall from collapsing under its load, and the infill was mortared. Wood strips, furred on the interior side of the wall, provided nailing surfaces for plaster lathes. In the second half of the nineteenth century, brick replaced the stone infill behind the facade stones. The bricks formed load-bearing walls that supported wooden floor beams and roof framing carried in interior wall pockets. By the turn of the twentieth century, new construction materials came into use. Steel beams and poured concrete made stone obsolete for structural purposes; its role became one of decorative cladding. One method of construction placed the facade stones in reusable wooden molds with poured concrete backing them to take the place of stone or brick infill. Today, due to construction techniques and the need for better insulation, stone is used primarily as cladding.[3]

EARLY STONE HOUSES

The message of the stone houses of the seventeenth and eighteenth centuries tells of durable material, conveniently procured under primitive conditions, which material was handled with little or no imagination or grace but with honesty and with a certain inherent propriety and suitability. The stone houses, however crude, are never vulgar and almost invariably fit their setting.

—HELEN WILKINSON REYNOLDS,
Dutch Houses in the Hudson Valley Before 1776, 1929

The diversity that has always characterized stone dwellings began with the earliest immigrants as various groups brought individual European masonry traditions and styles from their respective homelands. In St.

Augustine, Florida, the Spanish built houses of coquina, a shell aggregate limestone; in New York, New Jersey, and southern Connecticut, the Dutch built stone farmhouses and barns with flared gambrel roofs; in Pennsylvania, Germanic groups built distinctive stone bank houses and barns. Each group put practical experience and common sense to work in conjunction with their skills, available material, landscape, climate, and culture.

Until the mid-nineteenth century, American stonemasons used only the most accessible stone. In New England, the first stones the pioneers used were those left by the glaciers, irregularly rounded boulders of all sizes found on the surface of the soil. Moving them was slow, backbreaking work, something farmers wrestled with for years as they attempted to clear fields to plant more edible crops while the freeze-thaw cycle continually forced more stones to the surface. With labor at a premium and the rounded stones not particularly suitable for house construction, settlers generally confined them to foundations, chimneys, and fences. Where good building stone was found, however, stone house construction flourished at all levels of society. In the mid-Atlantic colonies—New York, New Jersey, Delaware, Maryland, and Pennsylvania—stones were angular and bedded in strata that broke naturally at vertical joints. This layered rock, easily mined by a few men and laid as it was bedded, was appropriate for house building. In addition to gathering loose stone from the surface of the land, settlers used picks and axes to quarry stone that lay near the surface. For deeper quarries, they employed terracing and channeling, methods dating back to the ancient Egyptians, Greeks, and Romans. It is not surprising to find that a list of early sandstone and limestone quarries, from 1639 to about 1800, shows that most existed in areas known for stone houses—New York, New Jersey, and Pennsylvania.[4]

Settlers came to the mid-Atlantic region from all over Europe, contributing to great cultural and religious diversity. The best masons came from countries with few trees, such as Holland, parts of Germany, Switzerland, France, Scotland, Ireland, and areas of England. And in the mid-Atlantic colonies they found abundant stone to adapt to their skills. New York settlers replaced early wood-framed houses with stone or brick as quickly as possible. In the seventeenth and eighteenth centuries, stone was generally used in the Hudson River counties from Albany County to Westchester and westward on the Mohawk in Schenectady County.[5] In Ulster County, French Huguenots, who had sought religious freedom in Holland, joined with Dutch immigrants in the late seventeenth century to settle in the valley between the Catskill and Shawangunk Mountains. There they found beds of blue sandstone that split easily along naturally divided vertical and horizontal joints, and beginning in about 1665, they used it to build rectangular stone houses uniform in size and style.[6] Although these like houses were originally thought to have been a frontier response combining masonry skills with local stone deposits and the tradition of medieval styles, people coming to this area continued building similar stone houses for almost two centuries, long after European traditions had been assimilated into standardized construction practices, and several are still occupied today. Indeed, stone house construction continued throughout New York's architectural history in various folk forms as well as in formal houses designed by well-known architects.

If New York had its fair complement of stone houses, Pennsylvania was identified with them. Pennsylvania and the Delaware Valley offer a good example of the combined effect of tradition and local material on the house types that settlers built. In the 1680s, immigrants from all over Europe were attracted to William Penn's commitment to religious tolerance and to peace with the native peoples, policies that contributed to the colony's success. People of Germanic heritage represented a major contingent of these immigrants, bringing with them a masonry tradition dating back to the Roman Empire. With stone easily quarried and lime readily available for mortar, stone was the colony's most common medium of construction.[7] The Hans Herr house, a folk dwelling in the medieval style dating from the 1600s, is the earliest surviving Pennsylvania stone house. Philadelphia, the social and business center of the colony, had its finest architecture. The most imposing houses were either stone or brick. In the surrounding countryside, the rich farmland attracted numbers of Germans and Swiss who built solid fieldstone houses with steeply pitched roofs reflecting the medieval styles of northern Europe. Early log houses were quickly replaced with permanent stone houses, the material favored by the rural Germanic gentry. Stone was used to build practical structures such as bank-sited houses and barns with a room dug into the slope for cool food storage.

As the population of the American colonies increased, people began moving into new territory in search of more land. By the 1750s, German-speaking people had reached the Shenandoah Valley, Virginia's western frontier. They took advantage of the plentiful local limestone to build houses that blended their own vernacular features with those of the Georgian style as it became fashionable. The houses were distinguished by their skilled stonework. Some were surrounded by palisades and used as forts where settlers could seek refuge from Indian attacks, still a threat in that territory. About thirty of these houses have survived.[8] Germanic stone house types are found as far south as North Carolina and as far west as Kentucky and Tennessee, testifying to the movement of these settlers—and to the availability of stone, prized much more for its permanence than the soft, porous local brick.

Not all German stonemasons were voluntary immigrants, however. In Virginia, a group of Hessian prisoners of war had been brought to Winchester and chose to stay on after the Revolution. In the 1780s, the area that is now Clarke County in the lower Shenandoah Valley also saw an influx of Tidewater families seeking new productive land and escape from the Tidewater climate. By the 1790s, architecture in Clarke County reflected the progression of housing concerns from those of practical function to those of form and style. Accustomed to the stately life of Tidewater mansions, many new residents built Georgian colonial houses to match their ancestral homes. The larger houses, such as Annfield, were built of limestone quarried on the property. Aware of the German talent for masonry, it is said that prosperous owners pressed the Hessians into service (albeit for wages) to do the stonework for their impressive houses.[9]

In contrast to the mid-Atlantic states, New England was settled predominantly by middle-class yeoman families from East Anglia. Although forests in England had become depleted by the seventeenth century and lumber had ceased to be economical, these immigrants had continued their tradition of heavy timber framing. Disembarking into the wooded wilderness of New England, they were astonished at the forest all around them and seized upon the wood for their most pressing need, shelter. The houses they built were folk imitations of the medieval architecture they had known in England.

Annfield, late Georgian colonial, Clarke County, West Virginia, 1790

Henry Whitfield State Museum, Gothic style, Guildford, Connecticut, 1639

Stone ender house, Lincoln, Rhode Island, 1687

As time and improving social and economic conditions allowed more formal architecture to replace the seventeenth-century houses, however, with few exceptions stone was little used. Nevertheless, it is evident in some of Boston's more imposing Georgian colonial houses that stone with its implications of great expenditures of time and labor was valued as a statement of success. Wealthy merchants built houses with wood framing made to look like stone through beveled edges and carved vertical scoring that was painted white to simulate mortar joints. Wooden imitations of stone quoins were added to corners. The siding itself was painted stone gray, and the quoins and keyed lintels, marble white. But in spite of stone's status appeal, New England's abundant forests made wood the obvious choice for houses, as it is today.

Some rare New England stone exceptions did exist, however. One of these, and the oldest remaining, was the 1639 Henry Whitfield House in Guildford, Connecticut. Built by a group of Puritans who sought religious freedom in the new world, the house was constructed for Whitfield, the leading minister, and his family. However, rather than the permanence or status usually equated with the use of stone in domestic structures, the motivation here was defense. According to Michael McBride, curator of the Henry Whitfield Historical Museum, the Puritans were primarily concerned with protection from those the king might send to impose his authority and that of the Church of England. A secondary concern may have been the Dutch, who were established in Hartford and southern Connecticut. The Indians, by then small in number, had ceased to be a threat. Indeed, they are believed to have helped haul the stone from a nearby quarry. With its steeply pitched roof, gabled ends, and asymmetrical placement of windows, the fort-house is a fine folk example of British medieval architecture.

Rhode Island provided another exception to New England's wood houses. The stone ender, a vernacular house form characterized by massive stonework covering one gable end, originated there. Large deposits of limestone for mortar were discovered in the state in the 1660s, allowing more extensive masonry construction than elsewhere in New England. (Other coastal settlers had only oyster and clam shells from which to extract lime.) The stone ender started as a one-room wood-frame house with a large stone fireplace at one end. It was commonly enlarged by adding a rear lean-to room with a second fireplace next to the first. The combined stone chimneys were so wide that they covered the entire end of the house. The source of the form is believed to be sixteenth- and seventeenth-century Wales and northwest England, areas that sent a number of early settlers to Rhode Island.[10]

EIGHTEENTH CENTURY PROGRESSION FROM FUNCTION TO STYLE

The American colonies had become a rapidly growing outpost of the British Empire by the turn of the eighteenth century. On the Atlantic seaboard, mercantile and shipping towns were growing, and a middle class had developed to influence cultural and commercial affairs as well as building styles. As always, the architecture of England became the architecture of America, although styles took several years to cross the ocean and were subject to the interpretations of local builders. Georgian style, based on the Italian Renaissance and the designs of Palladio, permeated the colonies from the early 1700s until the Revolution and rep-

Cliveden, Georgian style, Germantown, Philadelphia, Pennsylvania, 1760s

Peter Wentz house, with pentice, Worcester, Pennsylvania

Stonehall, Greek Revival house, Marshall, Michigan, 1837–38

resented a final break with the medieval architecture of early settlement. Characterized by symmetry, formality, and dignity, it was interpreted by American carpenters through British pattern books that provided builders with measured drawings of classical details. Its influence could be seen in both the grandest mansions and the humblest farmhouses.

Regional differences in the Georgian were based on local materials, cultural patterns, and social attitudes. In Pennsylvania, where stone continued to be an important building material, interpretations of the style had somewhat heavier moldings and details than those built elsewhere in wood, doubtless reflecting the more massive quality of the stone. One of the finest of these is Samuel Chew's Georgian summer house, Cliveden. Built in the 1760s in Philadelphia's Germantown and memorialized as the site of a Revolutionary War battle, its construction is particularly interesting for the exaggeration of the house's three-story height through the use of progressively more thinly dressed stones from foundation to roof. Chew, a Quaker, modified the ostentation of the five carved stone urns that ornamented the roofline with a cladding of sober gray-brown local schist and unornamented lintels. The house exists today as a museum.[11]

Another regional variation stems from a large group of Pennsylvania settlers from the midlands of England; unlike their fellow citizens in New England, they were accustomed to masonry. They are probably responsible for the pent, a distinctive feature of Pennsylvania houses of the period. Called a pentice in England and commonly used in the midlands, it is an eave above the first floor windows that sometimes extends the length of the house and occasionally includes a pedimented section over the front door.[12]

Although the Revolution brought about a break with England, post-Revolution American architecture continued to follow the fashions of the mother country. From the Revolution until the end of the nineteenth century, styles went through extreme swings of fashion from classicism through a variety of picturesque styles and back to classicism, swings that are documented in stone houses.

The Neoclassical movement, which had developed in England and France in the mid-eighteenth century, began to make an impact on American design soon after the Revolution. The movement is divided into two stylistic periods: Federal style, from approximately 1780 to 1820, and Greek Revival, from about 1820 to the 1840s. Brick most often characterized the Federal houses; these differed from the Georgian in elements of proportion, scale, and ornament. Choice of material, however, was dominated by local availability rather than style, and many mansions were constructed of limestone and other local stone.

Greek Revival, based on the post-and-beam construction of Greek temples, gave rise to the gable-end house, which usually fronted on the street and was painted white. The style also had much in common with Georgian and Federal architecture. Building type and structural method were similar, as was, more importantly, reliance on classical design principles, although those of Greece rather than of Rome. With associations of Greece with democracy and the notion of one's home a temple, Greek temples sprang up all over the country. Based on stone models but generally interpreted in wood, nevertheless, where stone was a major medium of construction, Greek temples were built in that material. Whether stone or wood, symmetrical plans, classical orders and details, and qualities of serenity and dignity made the transition from colonial styles to the Neoclassical one of natural ease.

THE ERA OF STONE
IN THE NINETEENTH CENTURY

The Revolution brought an end to the relative simplicity of colonial life, and by the turn of the nineteenth century, a more diverse society was rapidly developing. The guarantees of the Constitution encouraged individual freedom and a break with the established conventions of colonial society. The works of artists and writers made people aware of the vastness and beauty of the American continent. Romanticism, which gave birth to the picturesque, had come to America from Europe at the close of the eighteenth century. With its appeal to the emotions rather than to the mind, it was quickly embraced by an expanding young society in search of forms expressive of the uniqueness of the nation. Nostalgia and forms from another time and place are Romanticism's hallmarks. Rather than the whiteness and smoothness of classic architecture, picturesque styles were irregular, their textures rough and their colors rich, warm, and dark.[13] In short, the very description of stone.

Romanticism and advancing technology became the forces that fueled the development of architecture throughout the nineteenth century and helped to speed the conquest of the wilderness.[14] By the 1830s, a cavalcade of Victorian styles began to parade through the century, styles to which stone was particularly suited. Prior to about 1840, local quarries and glacial deposits were generally able to meet the demand for stone, and it was seldom shipped great distances. But by mid-century, rail and shipping lines had woven a transportation network that reached into the hinterlands, and new waves of immigrants brought growing numbers of skilled masons and a supply of cheap labor. The diversity of stone construction that had begun with the first settlers grew rapidly as stone was shipped wherever it was wanted. And it was wanted by an increasingly prosperous mercantile class for elaborate new houses in the changing architectural fashions of the Victorian era. Gothic Revival, Italianate, Second Empire, Queen Anne, Romanesque, Tudor—the styles overlapped, incorporating features from outgoing styles with incoming ones. Stone construction prospered with the Romantic enthusiasm for nature and the qualities of form that characterized the picturesque styles—irregularity, variety, movement, roughness, intricacy.[15]

Castle Marne, Victorian house, Denver, 1890

The picturesque was greatly influenced by Alexander Jackson Davis's pattern books for villas and cottages. Published in the 1830s and 1840s, they differed from the earlier builders' guides in that they showed how a house should be shaped rather than merely how it should be detailed. Davis deplored American domestic architecture and its classical styles, particularly their lack of connection to the site. His books inspired picturesque revivals of European architecture such as the Gothic Revival. Together with the Italianate it succeeded in overturning the order, balance, and whiteness of Greek Revival. Interest in how a building related to its natural setting made the use of stone particularly appropriate. Dark brownstone was well suited to the brooding Gothic Revival style in large country villas as well as in the small cottages that came to be designed specifically for the middle class.

Davis met Andrew Jackson Downing, architectural critic and landscape designer, in 1838. Davis's architecture and Downing's writings were to determine the direction of American domestic architecture between 1840 and 1875. Downing wrote that "architectural beauty must be considered conjointly with the beauty of the landscape or situ-

Italianate style house, Philadelphia, Pennsylvania, 1861

Lyndhurst (A. J. Davis), Tarrytown, New York, 1838, 1865

ation." Not only should the landscape be planned to enhance the house; the house should be designed to relate to its setting.[16] In his early books, Downing advocated building in stone for its naturalistic and historical qualities and opposed the imitation of stone forms in wood: "When we employ stone as a building material, let it be clearly expressed: when we employ wood, there should be no less frankness in avowing the material."[17] In 1842 he observed, "Stone is generally conceded to be superior, on the whole, to any other material for building. This is owing to its great durability and solidity, both in expression and in reality."[18] Wood, however, continued to be the more easily obtained and economical material, and Downing did adjust to its use in many smaller villas. Still, he did not completely give up his feeling for stone. He was opposed to white paint as too glaring against the soft green of foliage. In his 1842 publication *Cottage Residences*, Downing proposed instead a palette in "shades of gray . . . and . . . drab or fawn color, which will be found pleasing and harmonious in any section of the country."[19] At least one could have shades of stone, if not the material itself.

Stone, ever the status material, became the fashion in the large, formal houses of the rich along the Hudson River, something Downing approved: "A mansion may very properly have a graver color than a cottage, to be in unison with its greater dignity and extent."[20] Victorian authors compared the scenery of the Hudson River to that of the Rhine, and the rich were captivated by the notion of castles along the American Rhine. The mansions they built above the Hudson were local versions of the English Gothic manor house, the French chateau, and the castellated mansion—styles that virtually demanded stone. Writer John Zukowsky describes them: "Such rough-hewn stone villas with tall towers and flared roofs . . . were in keeping with Downing's recommendations for 'Rhenish' villas appropriate to typical Hudson River sites. Castellated mansions with their heavy masonry and forbidding parapets were not only evocative of ruins along the Rhine but, one might say, befitting of the robber baron status of some of their owners."[21] Many were designed by Davis; Lyndhurst is one of his most impressive. Turreted, crenelated, and parapeted, these early Gothic Revival modified castles were also designed by such other illustrious architects as Richard Morris Hunt and the New York firm McKim, Mead & White. Chateauesque mansions were built until about 1910 when once more classicism was to return.

While the rich were building castles along the Hudson, others—pioneers venturing into unsettled territories—built houses that adapted their needs for shelter to the climate and available material rather than to the changing whims of fashion. Their practical solutions have given them on-going life that would continue to interest architects more than a century later. While stone construction was a high-end endeavor in the ambitious houses of architectural taste, at the other end of the spectrum, stone was free for the gathering. Those accustomed to stonework took advantage of it.

For example, in the mid-1840s German immigrants began settling in and around the Texas Hill Country town of Fredericksburg. While the terrain at first seemed lush with green grass, the settlers soon found that it was growing on the hillsides in a thin, fragile layer of soil that wind and rain eroded within a season or two, uncovering the chalky white limestone just below.[22] Poor soil for crops, perhaps, but good material for houses, and for the next ten years or so the settlers put it to use. The writer Robert Caro describes those houses today, solid and still orderly over a hundred years later: "A surprise," he says, "to come upon after driving through miles of ramshackle scenery."

Norwegian immigrants, migrating from Wisconsin to Bosque County, Texas, also took advantage of the Hill Country limestone. They built approximately twenty houses between 1855 and 1885 in an area west of Fredericksburg. Markedly different from the German houses, in form and plan they bear a resemblance to the traditional double house design common in Norway. However, the settlers adapted their precedent to the Texas climate by including many windows and doors, and a wide breezeway separating the two-part house. Thus, they may have adapted their own traditional form to the Southern dog-trot dwellings.[23]

Some years earlier, in upstate New York, vernacular stone construction took another form. The first cobblestone house was built in the vicinity of Lake Ontario in the 1820s. Said to have been initiated by immigrant masons who had worked on the Erie Canal, cobblestone houses were built for the next forty years in an impressive array of styles and creative patterns. The uniform, water-rounded stones gathered from the lake shore were laid up with distinctive mortaring that set the stones off like jewels. The tradition spread south to the Finger Lake region and west as far as the Illinois-Wisconsin border. Within one generation, nearly one thousand cobblestone houses were built in colonial, Greek Revival, and Victorian styles.[24]

In Wisconsin itself, early architecture testifies to the existence of a rich variety of beautiful natural stone other than cobbles. Historic structures offer studies in the crafting of limestone, granite, and sandstone, work done by Cornish, Welsh, Irish, and German stonemasons.[25] It was here that Frank Lloyd Wright some years hence would take advantage of the mellow limestone to build Taliesin, his studio and home.

California also had its vernacular stone houses. In certain areas of southern California early in the twentieth century, before stucco there was stone, stone that was bountiful, durable, and available to anyone with a wagon to haul it away. The Arroyo Secco, a dry riverbed running through Pasadena and Highland Park and into Los Angeles, was the source for rather small, beautiful granite boulders that had been worn smooth by the river water that was once there. And so, like the cobblestone houses of upstate New York, the arroyo stone houses were built in a wide variety of styles—Victorian, colonial, classical, folk, even modern. Their construction ended when the 1933 Long Beach earthquake proved that the buildings that looked so durable were especially vulnerable to earthquakes.[26]

The Victorian era had its various styles to play out before the return to classicism at the end of the century. The late 1850s and the 1860s saw the decline of Gothic Revival and Italianate and the devolution of Second Empire, Queen Anne, Tudor, and Romanesque—styles that were often characterized by stone, carved and rusticated, ashlar and rubble. In the 1870s the noted architect Henry Hobson Richardson began designing houses that would come to be called Shingle Style, which featured a covering of shingles wrapped smoothly around corners and towers and over roofs in one continuous envelope. Although primarily a style of wood, rubble stonework was frequently used in stabilizing foundations and in chimneys. Often it was incorporated in the entire first floor of the house, grounding it more firmly to its site. In the 1870s, Richardson also designed urban structures in the Romanesque style, one of great power and sculptural beauty based upon the textures

Baker Cottage, Gothic Revival cobblestone house, Macedon, New York, 1850

Detail of cobblestone on Baker Cottage

of stone. Massive rusticated ashlar stonework and powerful half-round arches were the buildings' outstanding characteristics. At the same time, in his residential designs he looked to the land for inspiration, experimenting with geologic imagery. He used piled boulders and stones to create natural building forms. In 1880, these house designs culminated in the Ames Gate Lodge, which brought to the attention of American architects, as historian Vincent Scully describes it, "the expressive possibilities inherent in construction with rough stone, up to boulder size . . . In a poetic sense the Ames Gate Lodge represents an investigation into the primitive nature of a material." Henry-Russell Hitchcock said of Richardson that he "seemed to be seeking his inspiration back in the time before architecture took form."[27] Expensive to build, Richardson's work had a major, if short-lived, influence throughout the country, declining in the 1890s.

Ames Gate Lodge (H. H. Richardson), North Easton, Massachusetts, 1880–81

As the Romanesque style faded—and the Victorian era along with it—architects consciously rejected the picturesque styles. In 1893 the World's Columbian Exposition in Chicago regenerated interest in classical and Renaissance forms, as well as a new interest in America's own colonial past. Led by the influential firm of McKim, Mead & White, design returned to the kind of formal order and symmetry that had gone out with Greek Revival. The trend was equally influenced by the principles of the Ecole des Beaux-Arts. Once again architects made extensive use of stone. From about 1885 into the 1920s, ashlar stone, particularly white limestone or granite, characterized the facades of impressive residences built in the elaborately ornamented Beaux-Arts style.

THE TWENTIETH CENTURY: REVIVAL STYLES, PRAIRIE SCHOOL, MODERNISM

The early twentieth century introduced a period of strongly contrasting stylistic currents in domestic design. Many architects were designing houses in the revival styles—French, Spanish, Italian, Tudor, colonial. At the same time, Frank Lloyd Wright was designing houses that initiated the Prairie school, while in California contemporaries of Wright's were originating the Craftsman school. And in addition, the modern movement was beginning to gain momentum.

From 1900 to the 1940s, fashionable architectural firms used revival styles to design estates for well-heeled clients, with Tudor Revival and colonial styles rivaling each other in popularity. Historian Mark Alan Hewitt observes that thousands of Tudoresque houses, with half-timbering, rustic stone, and a medieval quality, were built between 1880 and 1940 throughout America. They were first built in country club communities outside major cities, such as Greenwich, Connecticut, the Main Line, extending from Philadelphia, and Lake Forest, Illinois, by the wealthy seeking "the flavor of antiquity and deep English roots." The Tudor Revival later expanded into subdivisions and garden communities as the style became popular with builders and mail-order catalogs. "Philadelphia's garden suburbs are particularly rife with examples of Tudor-inspired architecture, featuring the region's distinctive building stone, Wissahickon schist," Hewitt observes. "Tudor houses carried the cachet of expensive materials—copper, slate and especially stone."[28] By about 1920, the technique of veneering stone on wood-framed walls meant less costly construction, allowing smaller versions of the revival styles to be built in middle-class suburbs throughout the country, a

Tudor Revival house, Summit, New Jersey

trend that continues to this day, if in something of a pastiche of lamentably derivative architecture and wallpaper-thin veneering.

At the same time that revival styles were in fashion, a period of romantic eclecticism grew from an identification with indigenous American culture. As people traveled to new places in search of greater economic opportunity, an awareness of regional cultures and vernacular buildings developed. Hewitt compares the designs of McKim, Mead & White, taken from French chateaus, English country houses, and Italian villas, to "the regionalist architects [who] applied ornamental and typological elements from American vernacular sources to new problems." Many of these architects were drawn to vernacular sources because of their practical building solutions. Hewitt observes: "All regionalists were motivated by the powerful connections between style, building technics, materials, and the ethnic groups who used them in their buildings," as a reference point to solve "a variety of modern problems."[29] The many stone houses built in the 1920s and 1930s by such architects as Harrie T. Lindeberg and the Philadelphia firm of Mellor, Meigs and Howe are good examples of this regionalism. They drew on the simple early buildings of rural Pennsylvania and Delaware "as analogies to the village farmhouses of rural England," combining their basic massing and the distinctive local schist with a sensibility borrowed from modern English work to create beautifully scaled and romantic traditional country houses suited to the tastes of prominent families of the day.[30]

In the early 1900s, Frank Lloyd Wright began designing residences that would become the first uniquely American architecture. Lying low on the flat Midwestern terrain, clean lined and free-flowing of plan, they appeared to grow organically from their sites. In Wisconsin Wright selected native yellow sandstone for Taliesin, his home and studio. The stone was laid up as he found it buried, in stratified layers. He formed the rooflines of the building to echo those of the landscape, famously saying that a building should be *of* the hill, rather than *on* it. During his career, particularly in the 1940s and 1950s, Wright designed a large number of houses using stone.

In California, the Craftsman designs of architectural firm Greene & Greene were also concerned with integrating building and site. Indeed, during the late nineteenth and the early twentieth centuries the attempt to resist the forces of industrialization and return to a human approach to architecture resulted in the Arts and Crafts movement and its use of stone, a material unsuited to machines. Greene & Greene's houses featured the simple beauty of natural materials—wood and stone. Stone was always laid in the rubble texture of rounded cobblestones. Craftsman bungalows in particular, dating from about 1900, were characterized by shingles combined with extensive rubble stonework on their ground floors, porches, and pillars.

Simultaneously, a completely different style of architecture was developing: modernism. Industrial technology was accelerating, standardizing and prefabricating building elements, a development that would revolutionize construction practices as well as architectural design. Later called the International Style, modernism rejected all historical reference. Modernist architects Mies van der Rohe, Walter Gropius, Rudolph Schindler, Richard Neutra, and Marcel Breuer, coming to the United States from Europe, influenced the aesthetic of early modernism, and by the 1930s, it was established. Author John Welsh observes that although the world economy was not flourishing in the mid-1930s, enough stock market and manufacturing successes in the preceding ten

Taliesin (Frank Lloyd Wright), Spring Green, Wisconsin, 1911

Four-square house of Craftsman influence, Blauvelt, New York, 1926

years had produced a new business class of European entrepreneurs who sought a way to make a statement about their wealth. "Modernism on the rise was the perfect vehicle." If they could not join the aristocracy with ancestral mansions, these new magnates could beat them with Mies van der Rohe and Le Corbusier modernist villas of unadorned, crisp white walls and all-glass facades. With the arrival in the United States of these architects came the modern villa. For the newly successful such houses offered architecture on the cutting edge through which they could set themselves apart and express their achievements.[31]

Although the machine dominated the 1920s, an interest in the vernacular also developed. Analogies were drawn between the simplicity of the folk forms and those of the machine. While stone was not a machine-friendly material, between 1930 and 1935 Le Corbusier built three vacation villas in the regional tradition of stone without forsaking his modernist ethos, houses that were to influence Marcel Breuer. Indeed, Breuer's willingness to use local stone and building techniques helped to introduce the new modernism to a broader population. When he came to the United States, Breuer maintained his interest in the vernacular forms of New England.[32] He employed stone in several houses in the modernist style, taking advantage of the material's geometry and precision of line in cubist massing. Breuer's use of stone merged these houses with the landscape, unlike the machine-inspired designs of the International Style, which produced the house as object on the land.

Many found these abstract expressions in concrete, glass, and steel sterile, especially in mainstream private residences. After World War II, architects and their clients became increasingly disenchanted with architecture that often failed to consider site, climate, and local materials. The postmodern era was ushered in as such leading architects as Louis I. Kahn, Eero Saarinen, and Robert Venturi began experimenting with alternative designs and approaches that broadened the base of the modern idiom. The rise of the historic preservation movement in the mid-1960s led to a revival of interest in American vernacular architecture. Once more, through the use of materials like stone, architects began to reflect the old relationships with the environment and the influence of natural settings, but without completely discarding the principles of modernism.

Today, in this era of postmodern diversity, many architects remain committed to the modernist ethic of the house as an object on the land. Others find inspiration in historic forms as they reinterpret vernacular vocabulary to create their own unique contemporary houses. Postmodernism has adapted modernist forms and materials to concepts of light, space, and setting. Interiors and landscapes merge, often through the interior use of stone. If modernism rejected ornament, postmodernism allows materials themselves to be the ornament. Welsh observes that the architectural diversity of the postmodern era has led to the destruction of modernism's supremacy and reflects wider sources of inspiration, allowing landscape, color, and natural materials to inform design.[33]

The booming economy of the 1980s and 1990s has created more wealth for more people to spend on their houses and has led to what one architect refers to as a golden age of building, and what even might be considered a new age of building in stone. Architects "have suddenly taken up the villa as a worthy vehicle for their skills,"

Welsh observes. "Now, the private house, with the right sort of client, can offer a level of experimentation and improvisation to rival the most high-profile university or office building. The right kind of clients have also begun to reappear, their renewed interest a result of new money, just like the 1930s."[34] However, many architects have a different view. They contend that it is not a question of money that inspires clients to want to build in stone; rather, it is a reaction to the shoddiness and impermanence that is so much of building today. They seek the solidity and permanence, the authenticity that is stone.

Architects have been working in stone to modify and complement the natural landscape for centuries. Its permanence has willed a legacy of historic examples from which to draw inspiration. Today's architects, creating their own unique expressions in stone, such as the houses in this book, participate in that continuum. Working in the present, referring to the past, they create for the future.

NOTES

1. E. M. Winkler, *Stone in Architecture: Properties, Durability* (3rd ed., Berlin: Springer-Verlag, 1994), 1.
2. Frank Lloyd Wright, "In the Cause of Architecture IV: The Meaning of Materials—Wood," in *In the Cause of Architecture: Wright's Historic Essays for Architectural Record*, ed. Hugh S. Donlan and Martin Filler (New York: McGraw-Hill, 1975, 1987), 179–86.
3. Gordon Bock, "Stone Houses," *Old House Journal*, July-Aug. 1991, 26–29 passim.
4. Harley J. McKee, *Introduction to Early American Masonry: Stone, Brick, Mortar and Plaster* (Washington, D.C: Preservation Press, 1973), 9–15 passim.
5. Helen Wilkinson Reynolds, *Dutch Houses in the Hudson Valley Before 1776* (Payson and Clark, 1929; New York: Dover Publications, 1965), 11–22 passim.
6. McKee, *Introduction to Early American Masonry*, 11.
7. John Milnes Baker, *American House Styles* (New York: W. W. Norton & Co., 1994), 44.
8. James C. Massey and Shirley Maxwell, *Old House Journal*, May-June 1996, back cover.
9. Mary Gray Farland, *In the Shadow of the Blue Ridge* (Richmond: William Byrd Press, 1978), 8–9, 40.
10. Myron O. Stachiw, *Old House Journal*, Nov.-Dec. 1995, back cover.
11. Kim Keister, "History Lesson: Samuel Chew's Cliveden," *Historic Preservation*, Nov.-Dec. 1993, 52.
12. Baker, *American House Styles*, 44.
13. William H. Pierson, *Technology and the Picturesque: The Corporate and Early Gothic Styles*, vol. 2 of American Buildings and Their Architects (New York: Oxford University Press, 1978), 4–21 passim.
14. Pierson, *Technology and the Picturesque*, 6.
15. Pierson, *Technology and the Picturesque*, 10.
16. Pierson, *Technology and the Picturesque*, 349–50.
17. Quoted in Pierson, *Technology and the Picturesque*, 408.
18. Quoted in Leland M. Roth, ed., *America Builds* (New York: Harper & Row, 1983), 157.
19. Quoted in Vincent J. Scully Jr., *The Shingle Style and the Stick Style: Architectural Theory and Design from Downing to the Origins of Wright* (rev. ed., New Haven: Yale University Press, 1971), xxxiii.
20. Pierson, *Technology and the Picturesque*, 408
21. John Zukowsky, *Hudson River Villas* (New York, Rizzoli, 1985), 11.
22. Robert Caro, *The Path to Power* (New York: Alfred A. Knopf, 1982), 11.
23. Kenneth A. Breisch and David Moore, "The Norwegian Rock Houses of Bosque County, Texas: Some Observations on a Nineteenth-Century Vernacular Building Type," *Perspectives in Vernacular Architecture* 2 (1986), 64–70.
24. Carl F. Schmidt, *Cobblestone Masonry* (Scottsville, N.Y., 1966); Robert W. Frasch, Olaf William Shelgren Jr., Cary Lattin, *Cobblestone Landmarks of New York State* (Syracuse: Syracuse University Press, 1978), 1–25 passim.
25. Richard W. E. Perrin, *Historic Wisconsin Architecture* (Wisconsin Society of Architects of the American Institute of Architects, 1960), 8.
26. Joseph Giovannini, "The Southland's Stone Age." *Los Angeles Conservancy News* 4, no. 1 (spring 1982): 1–4.
27. Scully, *Shingle Style and the Stick Style*, 91–92.
28. Mark Alan Hewitt, "The Other Proper Style: Tudor Revival, 1880–1940," *Old House Journal*, Apr. 1997, 30–37.
29. Mark Alan Hewitt, *The Architect and the American Country House* (New Haven: Yale University Press, 1990), 196.
30. Hewitt, *Architect and the American Country House*, 198.
31. John Welsh, *Modern House* (London: Phaidon Press, 1995), 8–10 passim.
32. William Jordy, *The Impact of European Modernism in the Mid-Twentieth Century*, vol. 5 of American Architects and Their Buildings (New York: Oxford University Press, 1972), 169–70; also Christopher Wilk, *Marcel Breuer: Furniture and Interiors* (New York: Museum of Modern Art, 1981), 142.
33. Welsh, *Modern House*, 18.
34. Welsh, *Modern House*, 10.

STONE BUILT

URBAN/SUBURBAN

Oh, how beautiful is stone, and how soft it is in the hands of the architect! And how right and beautiful a thing is his whole completed work! How faithful to stone, and how well it preserves the idea, and what shadows it makes.

—PAUL CLAUDEL

BOOTH/HANSEN

HOUSE OF LIGHT, Chicago, Illinois, 1984

The challenge to the architects was to create in a city house the two potentially conflicting elements of light and privacy. This design accomplishes both goals. Light infuses the house, horizontally through large windows front and rear and vertically from a skylight over the center stairwell. The rooms achieve privacy because they are set back from the facade.

The classical Indiana limestone house was designed, says architect Lawrence Booth, "to resonate and harmonize with its surroundings" in Chicago's Old Town, an area of stone and brick houses dating from the 1880s. He believes an understanding of the rules of stone and its character—"how it is cut and produced"—is necessary to using it today. He endeavors "to use the rules to orchestrate the material to make the use of stone possible."

While most neighboring buildings have side entrances, the architects chose a center entrance to take advantage of the building's width. Above the entrance, a large pane of glass admits a flood of light to the library yet provides privacy because it is set at the rear of a central balcony. Rooms at the back of the house also have large windows but are private because they are set behind a balcony or terrace.

ABOVE AND OPPOSITE: *The House of Light is separated from the street by a required fifteen-foot setback, which immediately creates a degree of privacy and allows for an entry garden. The facade is Indiana limestone with green granite windowsills and mullions painted gray-green to match.*

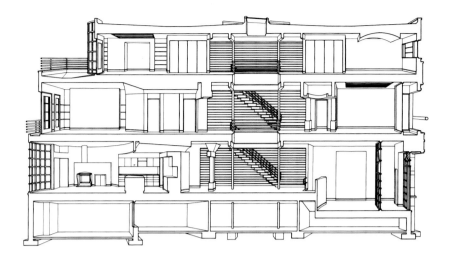

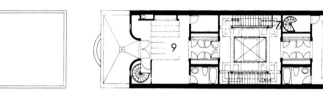

Third Floor

OPPOSITE: *An open, skylighted stairwell is at the center of the house. The ornament on the walls echoes the stair risers, "so cascading light could ripple down the walls," says Booth. Thirteen colors were used on interior walls and trim, each different but harmonizing with the others so that any two could be put together. At the front of the stairwell on the second floor is the library.*

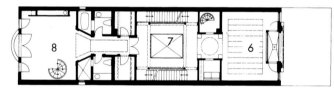

Second Floor

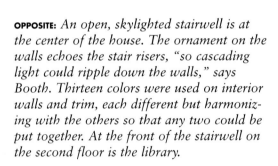

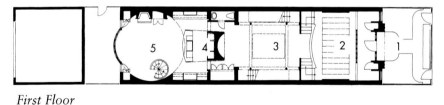

First Floor

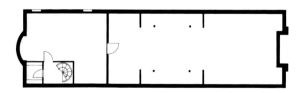

Basement

1. ENTRY
2. LIVING ROOM
3. DINING ROOM
4. KITCHEN
5. FAMILY ROOM
6. LIBRARY
7. ATRIUM/STAIRWELL
8. BEDROOM
9. MAIN BEDROOM

ABOVE: *The dining space on the first floor, directly under the skylight at the top of the stairwell, is elevated above a reception room, which mediates between it and the street. Facade fenestration admits light from the front, while the skylight directs light into the space from above.*
OPPOSITE: *At night the house glows with interior illumination.*

BUTTRICK WHITE & BURTIS
MANHATTAN TOWN HOUSE, 1993

ABOVE: *The Indiana limestone of the new facade creates a seamless transition to the neighboring limestone building.*
OPPOSITE: *The back facade of the house, made of brick and limestone, faces a garden.*

Built on the foundation of an 1883 row house, this elegant five-story town house is a welcome addition to a beautiful block in Manhattan's Upper East Side Historic District. With its new Indiana limestone cladding, the house is a good contextual neighbor to the two limestone facades to its west; together, they create a pleasing trio.

The architect, Michael Middleton Dwyer of Buttrick White & Burtis, designed the house, based on the Belle Epoque style of the late eighteenth century, for a couple with grown children. Before developing the plan and gutting the existing house, Dwyer held extensive consultations with the clients, who had very specific needs, including a dance studio for the wife, a steam room for the husband, a three-thousand-bottle wine cellar, and a garden designed for entertaining, as well as an appropriate setting for their collection of art, furniture, and decorative objects.

The new interior features a dramatic skylighted elliptical staircase that divides the house front and back, so that each room has the full width of the house. The ground floor accommodates at its center an oval faux-stone reception hall with a marble floor and an eighteenth-century French mantle. The kitchen is next to the entrance. The dining room at the rear opens onto a leafy garden that offers seclusion from the urban environment. Its brick facing trimmed with limestone blends with adjoining buildings. Other features include an elevator, four working fireplaces, and custom wrought-iron grilles and balustrades.

LEFT: *The piano nobile features a south-facing library and a formal north drawing room. "The woodworker had exactly enough French walnut on hand to panel the library," says Dwyer, who specializes in classical architecture.*
OPPOSITE: *The elliptical staircase that divides each floor is the most dramatic feature of the house.*
OVERLEAF: *The ground-floor reception room is of faux stone with a marble floor.*

1. MECHANICAL
2. WINE CELLAR
3. KITCHEN
4. ENTRY/RECEPTION
5. DINING ROOM
6. DRAWING ROOM
7. LIBRARY
8. DRESSING ROOM/STEAM ROOM
9. MAIN BEDROOM
10. GUEST ROOM
11. STUDY
12. DANCE STUDIO
13. STAFF QUARTERS

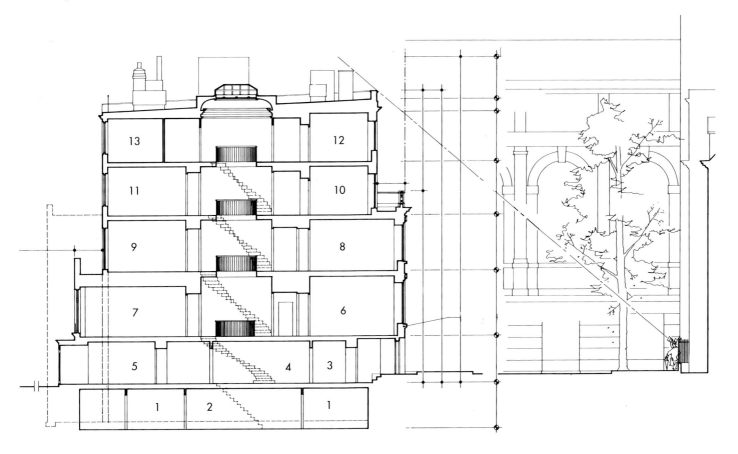

ABOVE AND PRECEDING PAGES: *The diverse rooflines and windows of this house evoke an Italian hilltop village. The clients were concerned about the ecological effects of construction, and so the separate pavilions are adapted to the site, varying in height and location depending on topography and existing trees. Vistas for both occupants and neighbors were preserved, and of the more than thirty trees on the site, only one was removed.*

With its varied rooflines and irregularly shaped and placed windows, it is difficult to determine whether this house is a historic building or a contemporary structure. The sixteen-room residence, located on a richly landscaped three-quarter-acre site, consists of seven distinct polygonal buildings connected by "meridians," spectacular metal-shingle-clad indoor corridors.

Clustered to resemble a small village, the design serves several purposes. Visually, it reduces the mass of what otherwise would have been a single large building; functionally, by creating one room per volume, it allows mechanical systems to be used as needed. Dividing the mass also maintained views and preserved trees for the benefit of neighbors and occupants. Materials used inside and out are almost as varied as the forms: in addition to the metal shingles, remnant granite blocks from South Dakota clad two pavilions. The stone, rejected for statuary, was "as economical as common brick," says architect Malcolm Holzman.

Minnesota limestone sheathes two other buildings and wood clapboards are used for the garage and a tower. The stone walls are thirteen inches thick.

Strategically placed windows create unexpected views of a specific tree or a glimpse from the inside of one pavilion to the exterior of another. A contemplation tower affords sparkling views of Lake Mendota. A third-floor studio provides a retreat for painting. The house may indeed evoke thoughts of "a tree house, an old stone castle, or a woodland cabin," Holzman notes. "The house is all these things."

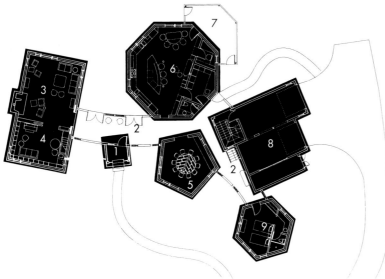

ABOVE AND RIGHT: *Granite clads the octagonal kitchen wing with its porch, and limestone wraps the living room volume next to it. Stone sheathes the pavilions inside as well as outside. The corner detail expresses the depth and mass of stone. "I believe in using stone the old-fashioned way—bearing on itself," says Holzman. The weight of each stone bears on the one below, unlike thin stone veneer, and the foundation is extended to carry the stone's weight.* **OVERLEAF:** *The kitchen, large enough for husband-and-wife chefs, includes informal living and dining areas.*

1. ENTRY
2. MERIDIAN
3. LIVING ROOM
4. LIBRARY
5. DINING ROOM
6. KITCHEN
7. GLASS PORCH
8. GARAGE
9. GUEST ROOM

ABOVE: *Meridians—interior corridors— connect the buildings. Floors are laid with sun-dried tiles.*
OPPOSITE: *The interiors are infused with natural light through roof fenestration and the strategic placement of windows, some near the floor for site lines to specific trees and*

others near the ceiling when only light and ventilation are needed. Each room is saturated with color, floor to ceiling. Only water-based paint was used.
OVERLEAF: *The windows, which vary in size and placement, are the most notable nighttime feature of the house.*

LAKE/FLATO

ELM COURT RESIDENCE, San Antonio, Texas, 1995

"The massive quality of stone is enhanced by using light-weight metal roof forms that sit on the blocks of Hill Country limestone," observes Ted Flato. The structures atop the pavilions are pyramidal shapes surmounted by steel cupolas, abstract lanternlike forms that, along with the clerestories, introduce indirect light to the interiors.

For this house, Ted Flato and his partner, David Lake, wanted to create privacy, a sense of space, and a connection to the outdoors, potentially conflicting goals given the city location. In addition, the client, a gallery owner, wanted space to accommodate her own art collection. To accomplish all this, the architects pushed the stone walls of the house to the lot lines and developed internal public and private spaces opening to courtyards.

At the center of the house is a thirty-foot-square sculpture courtyard, which is surrounded by a glass-enclosed art gallery that also serves as a circulation hall. At the corners are four pavilions containing the living, dining, and bedrooms and the kitchen. Each is just a single room deep for good light and cross-ventilation. Breezeways connect the rooms to the courtyards and the gallery, creating an inside-outside rhythm for occupants as they move through the house.

Metal and stone are common materials in central Texas, but in this house the architects have transcended their typical use with a modernist interpretation. To break down the scale of the walls they used limestone in large slabs, thirty-six inches wide and stacked only three or four to an elevation with thin, flush joints. Bands of gray stone add to the scale. The massiveness of the stone is complemented by metal roof structures.

Spanish and German immigrants to Texas built houses based on an innate understanding of climate and materials. Flato says, "It's not about romance. It's really about smart building. The climate, after all, hasn't changed in all this time. Our interest in vernacular forms is trying to do smart architecture for a particular place."

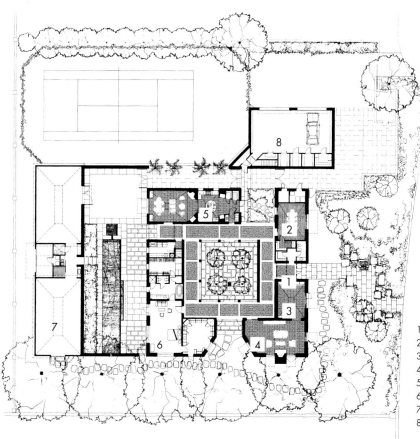

1. ENTRY
2. DINING ROOM
3. LIBRARY
4. LIVING ROOM
5. KITCHEN
6. MAIN BEDROOM
7. STUDIO
8. GARAGE

ABOVE: *The approach to the house is oblique, which shields it from the street, and is lined with crude blocks of marble, in contrast to the more refined but beautifully weathered limestone of the main facade.*

OPPOSITE: *A sunny, narrow pool courtyard separates the bedroom and kitchen pavilions from the studios. Clerestories provide diffused light for the owner's art collection.*

LEFT: *Above the doors to the main bathroom and the living room are galvanized steel gratings that will be covered with wisteria. Flato says, "They soften the walls and add energy, light, and air. Their lightness enhances the steel."*

OVERLEAF: *The art gallery/circulation hall encircles the central outdoor courtyard. Warm white oak floors contrast with banding of cooler Colorado limestone.*

LAWRENCE SPECK

HOUSE ON SUNNY SLOPE, Austin, Texas, 1989

In designing this house, Lawrence Speck, dean of the School of Architecture at the University of Texas at Austin, had in mind the compactness and irregular window placement of the simple nineteenth-century German stone cottages of Texas Hill Country. The wood siding of both the carport and the fence leads to the house, which is stone inside and out. A twelve-by-twelve-foot window opens the living room to the private front court; a stone wall mediates between the two. For this feature, Speck acknowledges a debt to a Luis Barragán building he saw in Mexico. "The drama of the enormous window in a stone wall is spectacular," says the architect. The owners particularly enjoy the combination of fireplace, window, and courtyard, plus an unexpected evening bonus: a view of the moon.

The thermal mass of the stone walls retains heat in winter and cool air in summer, keeping fuel bills very low. The walls, rather than being solid, have a cavity; this air space provides extra insulation. Speck's earlier renovation of a nineteenth-century house sparked the idea for this feature, which the architect enhanced with fiberglass insulation.

Speck describes the most important feature of the house as simply "feeling good." Part of that feeling he attributes to the stone. Stone, he says, can be bold and strong, or it can be intimate, as it is in this house.

ABOVE: *The module of the steps leading to the loft above the kitchen is also the module of the wrought-iron handrail.*

OPPOSITE AND PRECEDING PAGES: *The enormous window is the most striking feature of the facade at any hour; at night it becomes a lantern.*

Loft Level

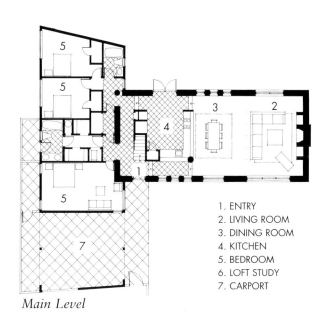

Main Level

1. ENTRY
2. LIVING ROOM
3. DINING ROOM
4. KITCHEN
5. BEDROOM
6. LOFT STUDY
7. CARPORT

ABOVE AND OPPOSITE: *To keep the stone walls intact, Speck created a freestanding structure in the living-dining wing to house the kitchen. He describes this as "either a very large piece of furniture or a small building." The cement column supports the loft study and bath above.*

LAWRENCE SPECK

CABLE LIBRARY ADDITION, Austin, Texas, 1983

The clients—a professor of English and a fine arts librarian—needed housing for their extensive collection of books. With architect Lawrence Speck, they explored historic forms, particularly Romanesque ones. The three found several examples of freestanding polygonal religious pavilions, such as baptistries, that seemed a good analogy for their purpose: a reliquary for books.

The library, an octagonal tower, stands on a beautiful site at the crest of a hill surrounded by trees. The freestanding tower, clad in mellow Texas limestone and pulled away from the house's front facade, rises twenty-eight feet. The use of stone adds to the sense of the library as a religious structure. Speck says, "Obviously I am fond of this stone. It is very beautiful in the outcroppings and cliff faces one finds frequently in the ragged, characterful central Texas landscape. Its soft, creamy color weathers beautifully here, picking up greens and grays and rust colors over time."

LEFT: *"The location of the trees was the controlling influence in siting the library," says Speck. "The tower is the shape of the trees in reverse, narrowing at the top as it rises into the foliage."*

THIS PAGE AND OPPOSITE: *Exterior cladding of split-face limestone from a nearby quarry was laid rather roughly to emphasize the rich texture of the soft, porous material. Additional stone for the interior fireplace came from the site itself: a hill of limestone covered with a shallow layer of grass, topography characteristic of Texas Hill Country.*

BELOW AND OPPOSITE: *Extensive wall space was the most important requirement for the library, so fenestration was limited. Clerestory windows provide added light and airiness without taking space from the books. Double stairs ascending on either side of the passage connecting the library to the house allow access to books on higher shelves as well as to the balcony. The wife's collection of drawings was hung in shadowed areas.*

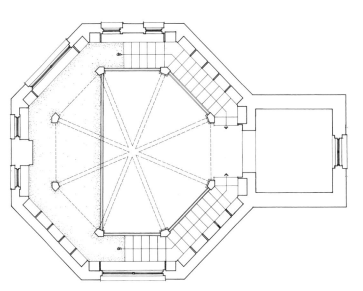

Loft Level

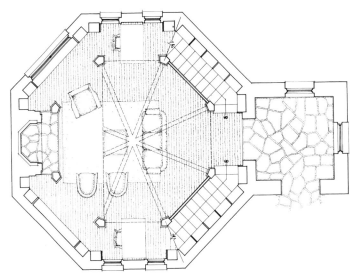

Main Level

TAFT ARCHITECTS

WILLIAMS HOUSE, Austin, Texas, 1987

At the time the three partners of Taft Architects, John Casbarian, Danny Samuels, and Robert Timme, designed this house in Austin, they had won a fellowship to the American Academy in Rome. Intrigued by the stone farm buildings of Tuscany, "we saw a similarity between them and some of Texas's stone houses," says Casbarian. "They generated ideas about the distinction between what is enclosed and what is not." The entrance to this house reflects that interest. One quadrant of the square plan is a grand double-height front porch, which creates a monumentality that makes the house appear larger than its 2,500 square feet. This illusion of scale, whether making a modest house seem larger or a grand house seem less imposing, is typical of the firm's work.

The corner site is delineated by walls of Austin limestone, which is characteristic of the older neighborhood in which the house is located. The stone encloses the street sides of the house, the garage/studio, and the garden. The challenge inside was to maximize the volume of the house for a young family of four. On the ground floor, the open-plan living-dining-kitchen space wraps around a central skylighted entry. Only the library and its state-of-the-art sound system are set apart from this sequence. Interior materials and colors reflect both the clients' and the architects' tastes and are used to reinforce the basic spatial organization.

BELOW, OPPOSITE, AND PRECEDING PAGES: *Because the initial concept was to use the limestone to anchor the corner, two walls of the local stone meet at the entry porch. The imposing walls continue to form both the garage/studio facade and the garden wall. Wood frames the remaining volume of the house. Square windows divided into smaller squares are a signature of the firm's work.*

ABOVE AND OPPOSITE: *An Arts and Crafts–influenced pergola shades the rear veranda. Stone piers and a semicircular planter use the limestone of the street facades. Three sets of doors extend the living space to the veranda and admit cooling summer breezes.*

BELOW AND OPPOSITE: *The interiors accommodate an eclectic collection of furniture and art acquired by the owners over a period of time. Marble-inlaid quarry-tile floors provide a sense of richness to otherwise simple and economical materials.*

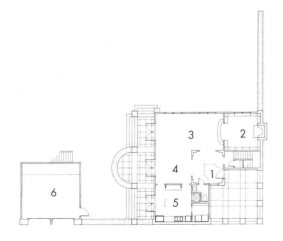

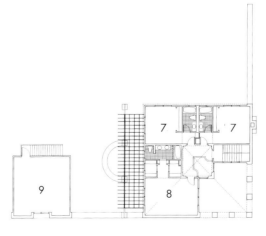

First Floor　　　　　*Second Floor*

1. ENTRY
2. LIBRARY
3. LIVING ROOM
4. DINING ROOM
5. KITCHEN
6. GARAGE
7. BEDROOM
8. MAIN BEDROOM
9. STUDIO

ABOVE: *The main rooms of the ground floor and stairs leading to the three bedrooms on the second floor are organized around the entry.*

RIGHT: *The entry space is capped with a translucent fiberglass skylight that allows regulation of the ultraviolet rays flowing into the house.*

COUNTRY

The stone and wood, not bought but found, are used true to the rights one dares to take in gratitude from the gifts of nature. These noble and most ancient materials which in all ages inspired numerous and beautiful variations in the expressions of their order here were used true to their nature with clarity and economy.

—LOUIS I. KAHN, *The Hill Country Revisited*

1100 ARCHITECT

RESERVOIR HOUSE, Westchester County, New York, 1994

Before 1100 Architect began a renovation of this house in Westchester County, all that was visible from the road was the roof. The structure had begun as a fieldstone caretaker's cottage on a steep hill overlooking a small wooded lake. Over time, a number of additions, some wood framed, were built further down on the slope. The clients wanted the existing structures renovated for use as a main bedroom suite and guest quarters and a two-thousand-square-foot addition constructed for the public functions of the house.

Design partner Juergen Riehm says, "It was very important to integrate the house with the landscape as well as with the existing structure." To achieve this integration and to make the addition appear as though it had always been there, architects and clients chose to continue the fieldstone of the original cottage. Formally, the addition is a house that steps up to road level, creating a presence at the end of the long driveway. Containing large living and dining rooms and the kitchen, the addition nevertheless appears as a small, rather modest house, something the clients particularly appreciate.

The architects had the good fortune to find the local quarry used in building the caretaker's cottage, and the contractor hired an experienced Italian mason. "What the clients liked about the old structure was the tight joints, slightly set back, so you get shadows," says Riehm. "It's important that workers know the material and bring out its small details." The quarried stones, six to ten inches thick, were carefully broken and stacked to avoid the look of thin flagstone veneer.

OPPOSITE AND PRECEDING PAGES: *The low spreading roof, with an overhang reminiscent of Frank Lloyd Wright, appears as though it is a separate element, as though it is floating. To accomplish this, the architects introduced a neutral band of stucco at the top of the stone wall, separating stone and roof.*

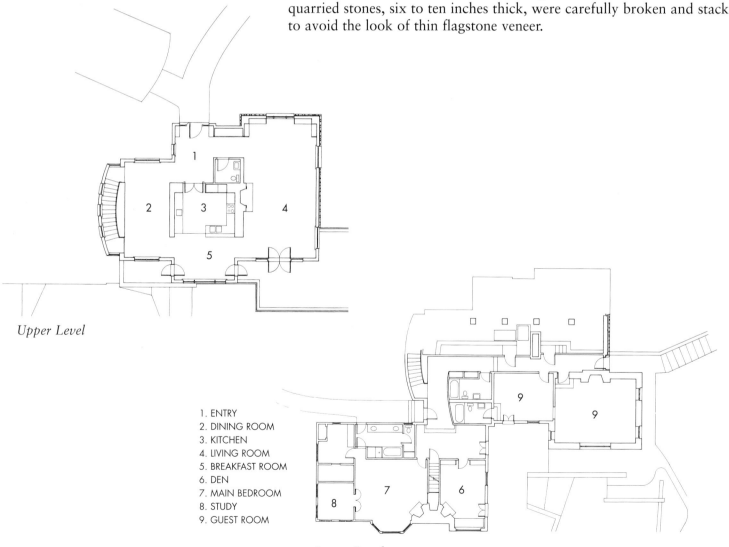

Upper Level

1. ENTRY
2. DINING ROOM
3. KITCHEN
4. LIVING ROOM
5. BREAKFAST ROOM
6. DEN
7. MAIN BEDROOM
8. STUDY
9. GUEST ROOM

Lower Level

THIS PAGE AND OPPOSITE: *Kitty Hawks designed the beautifully proportioned rooms of the interior. The living room incorporates an open ceiling, suggesting a barn—a very refined barn. The barrel ceiling of the dining room creates a sense of unbroken height, contributing to its spaciousness.*

OVERLEAF: *The design successfully integrates the original buildings on the site, the addition, and the landscape, bringing cohesion and intimacy to an assemblage whose former distinction was primarily the splendid site. "Previously, only one room had a view of the lake. Now the upper house has a view from all its rooms," says Riehm.*

The site and the clients' needs dictated the form of this house on the edge of a mountain preserve overlooking Paradise Valley and Phoenix. The owners wanted an adult retreat with room for visiting children. They also wanted a house that was at once luxurious and modest in scale. To meet these challenges and to focus on the views, Will Bruder developed a 3,500-square-foot, open-plan, triangular residence.

Stone for the house came from a canyon that had been carefully cut into the mountain for a minimum of environmental disturbance. Rubble stone culled from the excavation was used for walls that wind sinuously out from the copper and glass "hang glider" form of the house. The monolithic walls provide platforms for the outdoor terraces, pool, and hot tub. Bruder enjoys the rigor of laying the stone with fine jointing so that color and pattern dominate. The materials articulate a composition that virtually disappears into its site, minimizing visual impact from a distance.

The self-educated Bruder, who has a degree in sculpture, is part of an American tradition of architecture influenced by Frank Lloyd Wright and Bruce Goff. From Goff, whom he knew, Bruder says he learned about the power of listening to the clients and celebrating them with architecture. "I'm allowed to do all of the hopefully wonderful, hopefully strange, hopefully inventive things I do because of my clients," he says.

The architect describes the house, often referred to as the "copper-clad cabinet," as a treasure chest that grew from the mountain in both its rock-like angular form and its color. In the arid climate, the patina of the copper will retain its purple-bronze tones, matching the burnished colors of the native stone and integrating "in a very soft way with the desert."

OPPOSITE: *Smooth white oak paneling and cabinetry are juxtaposed with rough resawn-fir ceilings. Inset into the sandstone floors of the dining and living spaces are area rugs. Furnishings are simple, strong, and few; the architect was involved in every detail, down to the choice of telephones and linens.*

PRECEDING PAGES: *Serpentine stone walls contrast with the angular character of the central portion of the house.*

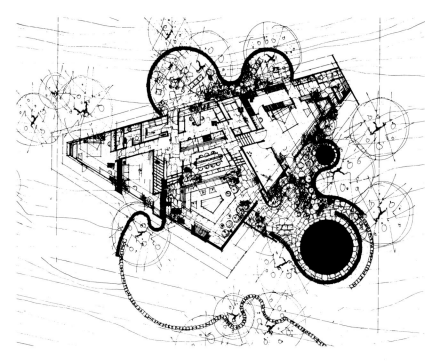

ABOVE: *Bruder, who is greatly influenced by ruins such as the great prehistoric Native American sites, says, "Stone is so much a part of the geology of place. The western United States, with its young mountains, is a great source of it." He likes to use stone as an anchor to the ground as well as to incorporate it into indoor-outdoor contexts— "Wrightian roots of mine," he comments. In the main bath a mountain outcropping was left in place, its ledges ideal for plants that benefit from the humidity.*

RIGHT: *A seven-foot-square white oak door pivots into the entry. Burnished copper elements contrast with the flagstone on the stairs, which lead to the living space and its explosion of views. The house was built around a rocky outcropping of the mountain, seen at the rear of the photograph.*

DEAMER + PHILLIPS

RICH RESIDENCE, South Hamilton, Massachusetts, 1990

BELOW AND RIGHT: *Sited on a flat area of the wooded lot, the orientation of the house was determined by the sun. The glazed corridor faces south, toward the most desirable views.*
PREVIOUS PAGES: *The guest house is directly north of the bedroom wing.*

Seventeenth-century New England houses never reached the size of seven thousand square feet. Nor were many of them clad in stone. Nevertheless, this residence is strongly evocative of early vernacular New England structures. The simplicity of the geometric forms, the small, widely spaced windows, the prominence of the chimneys, and the precision of the stone cladding give the structures an archetypal quality. Yet the architects, Scott Phillips and Peggy Deamer, created a design whose strong, clear forms are in essence modernist.

The owner, a masonry contractor, wanted a house that would accommodate his large, extended family. The architects reduced the scale of what would otherwise have been a massive house by separating the living spaces from the bedrooms and building separate structures for the garage and guest house. These simple forms were arranged in a T shape, creating two courtyards.

The house was framed in wood with insulation and clad in stone—economical six-inch-thick granite tailings from a curbing quarry. Unlike veneer, the stone sits on an extension of the foundation; it bears on itself and is tied to the frame with metal clips.

A south-facing glazed corridor extends the breadth of the living spaces. Separated from them by stone columns, it functions as both circulation space and porch. A series of glazed doors along the corridor opens the rooms to summer breezes and admits warming winter sun.

ABOVE AND OPPOSITE: *Architect Scott Phillips describes the stonework, done by the owner, as meticulous: "It was done with exquisite precision and provides texture and variety as well as conveying a sense of solidity and permanence." The entry to the complex is between the guest house and the bedroom wing; the entry to the main house is between the bedroom and living wings.*

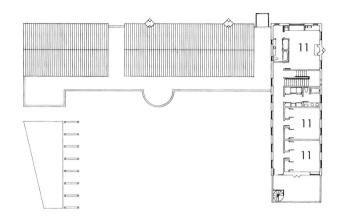

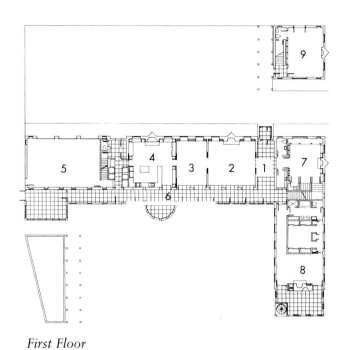

Second Floor

First Floor

1. ENTRY
2. LIVING ROOM
3. DINING ROOM
4. KITCHEN
5. GARAGE
6. GLAZED CORRIDOR
7. LIBRARY
8. MAIN BEDROOM
9. GUEST LIVING ROOM
10. GUEST BEDROOM
11. BEDROOM

ABOVE: *The public rooms, designed to accommodate many family members and guests, interconnect with each other and with the circulation corridor.*
OPPOSITE: *The library marks the junction between the bedroom wing and the living wing.*
OVERLEAF: *The glazed corridor, outside the stone mass of the house, is a place for both circulation and congregation. Its floors are polished granite.*

HUGH NEWELL JACOBSEN

BRYAN RESIDENCE, Butler, Maryland, 1987

When viewed from a distance, this fifteen-thousand-square-foot house creates the visual impression of an intimate collection of farm buildings, albeit farm buildings designed by a distinctly modernist hand. Because the house is broken into eleven pavilions, only a third of it can be seen from any single perspective. Indeed, even from within the occupants glimpse only portions of the whole.

The house is set on the crest of a hill at the end of a long driveway amid seventy-five acres of rolling Maryland countryside. The owners, a couple with grown children who visit with their own families, are able to accommodate a great many guests overnight, yet the house imparts a quality of closeness that overcomes the grandeur of its size.

It took three years of cutting and chiseling to lay the local fieldstone in its ashlar pattern. "It's like putting together a giant puzzle," says Jacobsen, who believes stone is the most desirable building material. Here the stone comes from the land; it defines the form; it *is* the architecture.

The living room is turned forty-five degrees to take advantage of the panoramic view of the countryside; it faces a distant church that has a steeple of the same Butler fieldstone. The other pavilions circle back from this focal point, creating both an entry courtyard (accessed through a porte cochere and with a magnificent copper beech in its center) and a pool terrace. The many parts are unified by the precise geometry of the slate roofs, the monumental verticality of the chimney masses, and the coursing of the stone.

BELOW: *The bridge above the porte cochere houses a guest suite—living room, bedroom, and breakfast room.*
OPPOSITE: *The pavilions are clustered around the entry courtyard, seen through the arch.*
PREVIOUS PAGES: *The pool terrace is on one side of the main bedroom; a view toward the living room is on the other.*

BELOW: *The kitchen is part of the large family room.*
OPPOSITE: *The main bedroom suite has views of meadow and green grass stretching to the brow of a hill. All rooms open to the landscape. Throughout the house, most carpets and walls are white, and the furniture, arranged symmetrically, is classically modern while bespeaking comfort.*

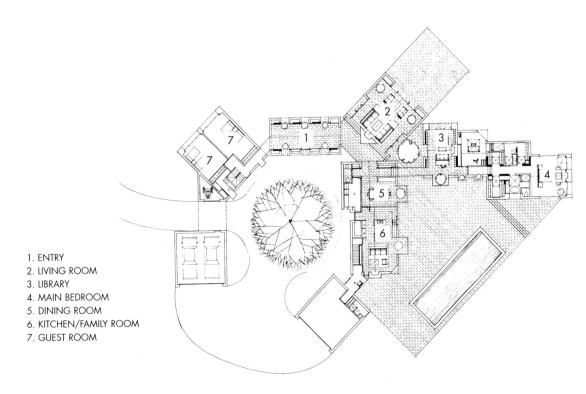

1. ENTRY
2. LIVING ROOM
3. LIBRARY
4. MAIN BEDROOM
5. DINING ROOM
6. KITCHEN/FAMILY ROOM
7. GUEST ROOM

ABOVE: *The entrance pavilion at the end of the long driveway is designed as a lantern, its windows aligned east and west to fill it with welcoming light. "I have always believed that a driveway is a roll of drums," says Jacobsen. "And you don't go through all that and not get a reward."*

OPPOSITE: *The entrance pavilion leads directly to the living room. "And then there it is," says Jacobsen. "My God, the church!" Stone flooring passes beneath the floor-to-ceiling windows to reinforce the vista as well as to merge the interior with the exterior. Diamond-shaped windows are a unifying element of the design.*

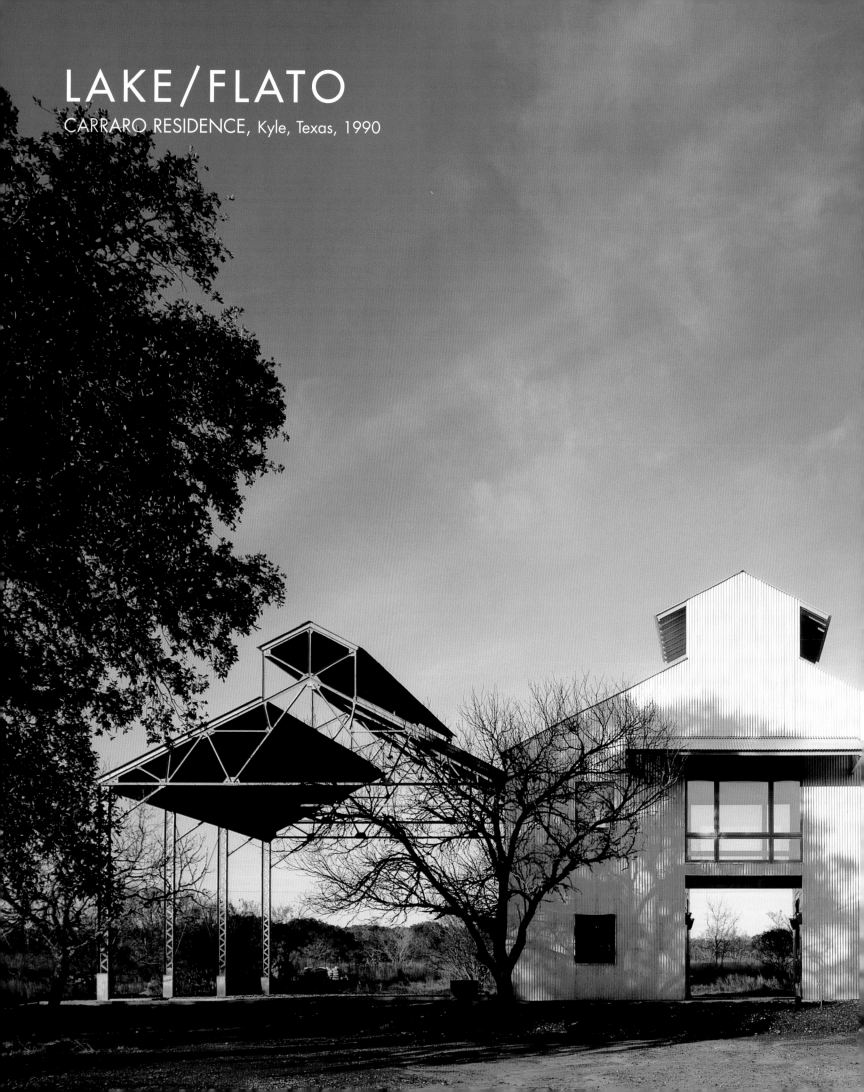

LAKE/FLATO

CARRARO RESIDENCE, Kyle, Texas, 1990

The clients came to Lake/Flato with "a wonderful spirit and a tight budget," says architect Ted Flato. They owned forty acres of scattered oaks and river-bottom land between Austin and San Antonio and wanted a big, flexible living space. When the clients' original thought of a stone barn proved too expensive, the design team of Flato, David Lake, and Graham Martin suggested recycling a concrete plant in San Antonio that was about to be demolished and sold for scrap, a building with rooflines the architects had long admired. "Industrial structures such as silos and cement plants are always delights," says Flato. "They're so straightforward and truthful, and they end up with interesting solutions that are not based on taste or anything else."

The 1920s metal building—40 feet wide, 20 feet tall, and 180 feet long—had delicate trusswork and columns built out of small steel angles. "We thought the trusses and columns were absolutely wonderful," says Flato. "They celebrate the lightness and beauty of steel." Recycling not only preserved their beauty but also created an inexpensive, spacious house. The architects broke the structure into three buildings to create outdoor spaces in the landscape. This Z-shaped arrangement forms courtyards on either side.

For the principal dwelling, the architects inserted a stone building to house living, dining, and kitchen spaces within the screened walls of the north structure. A metal-clad guest room is perched above it. The heaviness and permanence of the Texas limestone emphasize the light, lacy quality of the steel trusses and columns, and also offer protection from winter winds. The central building, clad in metal, has an open dog-trot entry (another vernacular form) to the main bedroom and library. The third pavilion serves as a garage.

OPPOSITE AND PRECEDING PAGES: *Among the vernacular typologies Lake/Flato draws from are industrial structures, buildings that are "trying to get away with the simplest solution to a problem," says Flato. An old recycled cement plant was divided into three sections and reassembled to create this house on a site bordered by large limestone cliffs and a small stream.*

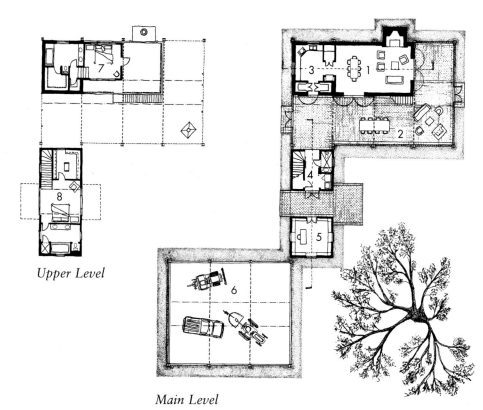

Upper Level

Main Level

1. LIVING ROOM
2. SCREENED AREA
3. KITCHEN
4. ENTRY TO MAIN BEDROOM
   AND LIBRARY PAVILION
5. LIBRARY
6. GARAGE
7. GUEST ROOM
8. MAIN BEDROOM

LEFT: *The massive weight of the limestone accents the delicacy of the metalwork of the old cement factory. Flato says of the trusses, "They're as light as a truss can be. They celebrate the beauty of steel."*
BELOW: *Galvanized corrugated steel sheathes the dog-trot entrance to the main bedroom and library pavilion.*
OPPOSITE: *The space outside of the stone building but within the screened structure is simultaneously interior and exterior.*

ABOVE: *The sheet-metal-clad guest room sits lightly on its stone base.*
RIGHT: *Recycled cement-kiln bricks line the vault of the fireplace inglenook.*

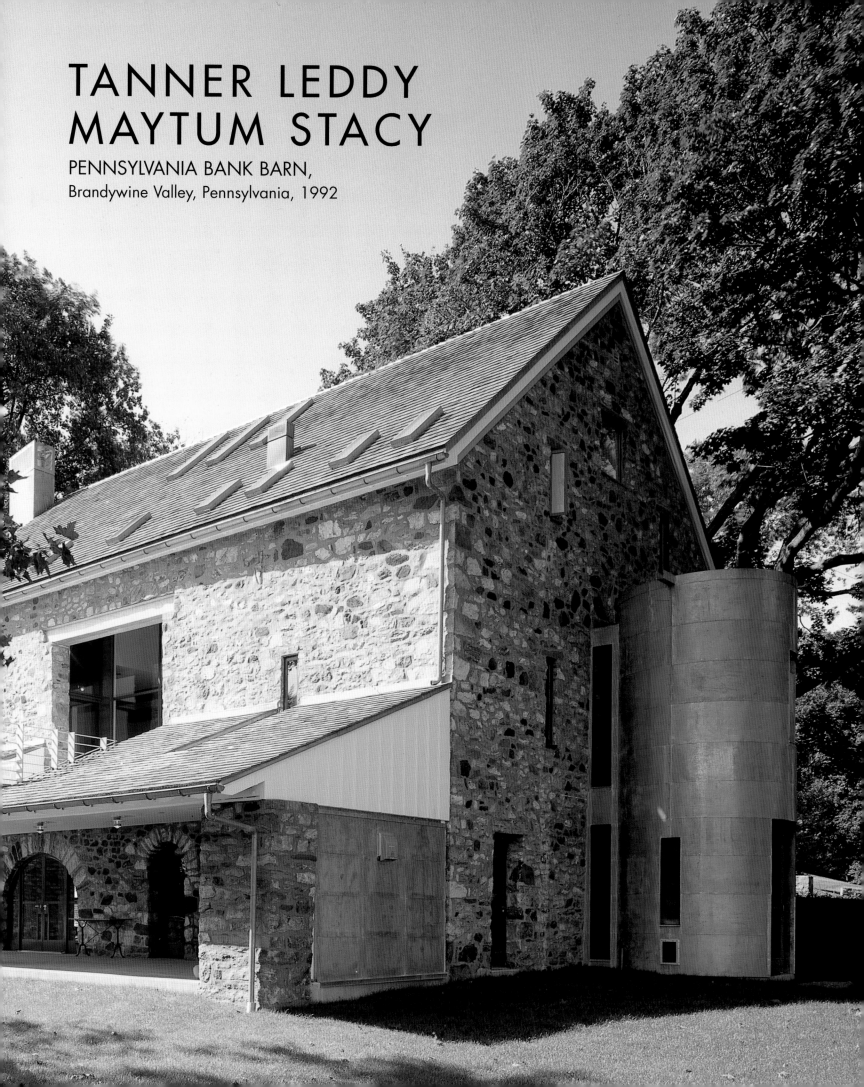

TANNER LEDDY
MAYTUM STACY

PENNSYLVANIA BANK BARN,
Brandywine Valley, Pennsylvania, 1992

n 1820, Amish masons built a large barn from local fieldstone. In 1992, as he converted the barn into a house, architect William Leddy strove to create a dialogue between the past and the present through design, so that the occupants could "feel on a day-to-day basis that they were engaged with the history of the place."

The clients wanted to expose as much interior stone as possible, which made it difficult to insulate the house. Further, the existing twenty-inch stone walls could not carry any additional loads. Leddy solved both problems by designing a "cabinet" of smooth cherry wood set three-and-a-half feet inside the stone walls that would support all new structural loads as well as provide insulation. The insertion also created a circulation space between new and old walls. As the occupants move through the house, they move between past and present, past rough stone to smooth wood, from old flagstone floors onto the smooth, waxed concrete of the cabinet.

The dialogue between past and present extends all the way through the house and continues outside the stone walls. To house the main bath, Leddy designed a galvanized-steel cylinder, drawing inspiration from a small silo on the property. He is interested in "the poetic and the pragmatic in architecture," and says that the project gave him a chance to "play with and marry the two."

BELOW: *A new opening and roof terrace— the only major change to the original walls of the barn—connect the living room to the outdoors and offer rolling countryside views.* **OPPOSITE:** *The cylindrical geometry of the steel silo form is a counterpoint to the Euclidean purity of the original building. Wind-eye windows were enlarged slightly and reglazed.* **PRECEDING PAGES:** *The barn—old and new— is protected by a low wall.*

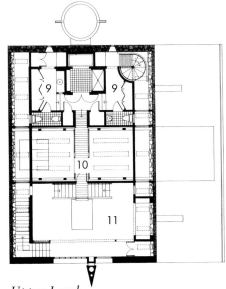

Upper Level

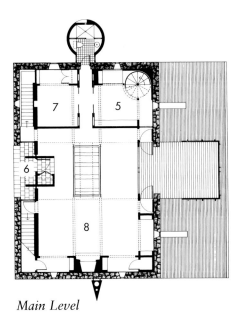

Main Level

ABOVE: *The entrance, on the main floor, is a single door set inside a metal-clad cube that delineates the original barn door. The new entry is low and intimate, providing a transitional space of reduced scale before opening to the generous space of the living room.*

OPPOSITE: *New metal posts meet original handhewn oak beams in the double-height living room. Steel surrounds an opening that admits light to the lower level.*

OVERLEAF: *The kitchen, dining room, and family room illustrate the dialogue between old and new. "Architecture," says Leddy, "is all about making connections. Stone connects to the making of the building—the human hand and the people who made it."*

SECOND OVERLEAF: *Seen from a distance, the house is hardly different from the Amish barn built in the early nineteenth century.*

Lower Level

1. MUD ROOM
2. DINING ROOM
3. FAMILY ROOM
4. KITCHEN
5. OFFICE
6. ENTRY
7. GUEST ROOM
8. LIVING ROOM
9. DRESSING ROOM
10. BRIDGE
11. MAIN BEDROOM

ALAN WANZENBERG

KENNELOT FARM, Connecticut, 1985

When Alan Wanzenberg first visited the site in the early 1980s, it held a collection of a half dozen decrepit, abandoned farm and residential buildings. Originally designed by Donald Barber in the early 1900s, they combined the Shingle Style and late-nineteenth-century Bracketed Queen Anne style; the fretwork and details on the balconies also suggested an Asian influence. "The buildings had great detailing," says Wanzenberg. "Enough of it remained to document and to employ in the renovation."

The original walls of the main house, approximately sixteen inches thick, are load bearing. They were built of stone quarried on the property after a small stream was excavated. The architect worked to preserve the exterior scale of the building, following what was there and using it as precedent in adding new elements. On the interior, he provided insulation by adding eight inches to the walls.

"We moved back and forth," Wanzenberg says, "from precedent to modernization. The client adored the outside of the buildings. They resonate with something very special in people, something poetic."

BELOW: *The old garage was converted into the main bedroom. Bracketing and Asian influences can be seen in the roofline and balcony detailing. The French doors are an adaptation of another element found in the original building.*
OPPOSITE: *The overscaled swing outside the studio has sweeping views of the property.*
PREVIOUS PAGES: *Old buildings on the site provided a template for the style and details of the new house.*

ABOVE: *The artist's studio, built in 1988, was added to a stone ruin that was left in place.*
RIGHT: *The interiors were designed by Parish Hadley. The large windows and French doors were suggested by elements in the original structures. Wanzenberg worked to preserve the refined scaling and detailing of the exterior, adapting them to the interior.*
OVERLEAF: *What were once decrepit farm structures now offer romance and a connection to the past.*

WATER

For in the stony bone-work of the Earth, the principles that shaped stone as it lies, or as it rises and remains to be sculptured by winds and tide—there sleep forms and styles enough for all the ages for all of Man.

—FRANK LLOYD WRIGHT, "In the Cause of Architecture"

BARNES COY
EASTERN LONG ISLAND RESIDENCE, 1996

The clients envisioned a house that would last not just a hundred years, but one that would still provide shelter at the end of the next millennium, solid and strong. Moreover, they asked for a house with low maintenance. In short, they wanted stone—inside and out.

The site presented to architects Robert Barnes and Christopher Coy had spectacular views over a Long Island bay. But it was burdened with a number of constraints—a property line setback, a conservation easement, and a scenic easement—that resulted in a small, linear building envelope. The architects responded by creating an arc, a tilted, long, thin, curving form that allows maximum water views. More subtly, the shape also recognizes the curvature of the earth. "The house has a hundred-year stare," says Coy. "Its eyes are fixed on the distant horizon."

The joints of the Pennsylvania limestone are thin, reminiscent of those of drywall construction, which reduces maintenance; other materials are glass, copper, and teak. A dramatic tension exists between the great expanses of glass and the massive, opaque stone structure that supports it. Stone piers and twenty-two-inch-thick walls appear to grow from the ground; as the topography changes, the stone follows it. "The glass," says Barnes, "puts you in the landscape; at the same time, you're sheltered by the stone."

BELOW: *From certain perspectives, the effect is one of ruins rising powerfully from the ground.*
OPPOSITE: *A tower clad in teak contains a library and a study—enclosed rooms that contrast with the openness of the living room.*
PREVIOUS PAGES: *The entrance facade of the house, primarily Pennsylvania limestone, is angular; entry is via a bridge.*
OVERLEAF: *The opposite facade is a striking glass curve atop a stone base.*

OPPOSITE: *The transparency of the living room is anchored by the massive stone fireplace. In winter, radiant heat in the floors and walls warms the house, while an ambient air system with louvers allows cool air to enter to balance excessive solar heat. In summer, motorized hatches in the roof and large windows open the house to breezes. The marble for the floors was quarried from the same Georgia vein that supplied the United States Capitol and the Lincoln Monument.*
OVERLEAF: *The glass of the windows becomes the dominant material in the evening.*

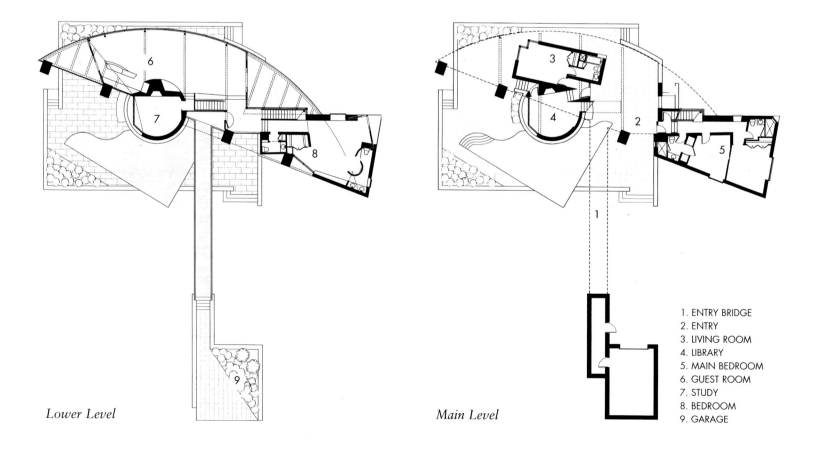

Lower Level

Main Level

1. ENTRY BRIDGE
2. ENTRY
3. LIVING ROOM
4. LIBRARY
5. MAIN BEDROOM
6. GUEST ROOM
7. STUDY
8. BEDROOM
9. GARAGE

BOOTH/HANSEN

HOUSE ON LAKE MICHIGAN, Highland Park, Illinois, 1995

The activities accommodated in this eight-thousand-square-foot lakeside house are as varied as the interests of the large and very active family occupying it. There is a movie theater, a game room, his-and-hers studies, an exercise room, indoor and outdoor swimming pools, summer bedrooms, a music space, a Japanese guest room—and a Lake Michigan beach only steps away. Imposing as the exterior of the house may be, the interior is intimate—the largest room is fourteen by twenty-two feet.

Architect Lawrence Booth strives for visual richness, and one way he achieves it is through varied materials, textures, and forms. Another way, especially in this design, is by providing a wide variety of options for looking. "It's a tapestry of proportion, of forms and light inside and out, so that as the occupants move through the house they continually find new vistas," he says.

Because the house is on the lake, the site was limited; the Chicago climate was also a consideration. Architects and clients chose ashlar limestone with fine joints for its low maintenance. Booth says, "Any time we can build in stone, we do. The challenge is to find strategies to make it possible. Large windows, for example, reduce the amount of stone needed for the walls."

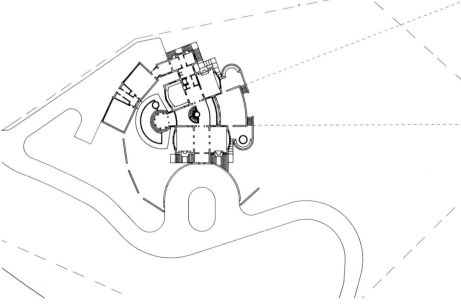

ABOVE: *The central hall and the principal rooms have large window bays, which fill the house with light and afford expansive views of the ever-changing waterscape.*

PRECEDING PAGES: *The architects used limestone in a variety of ways: rough contrasts with smooth, and quirky shapes with sheer surfaces.*

ABOVE: *The outdoor pool is an architectural garden sculpture, a folie with stone-capped, smooth stucco columns that play against the rough rockface walls of the garage. "The sun creates shadows for architectural texture when viewed from upper floors of the house," says Booth.*
LEFT: *The two main pavilions of the house face slightly outward, the better to encompass the sweeping views.*

ABOVE: *The music hall is between the dining room and the living room.*
OPPOSITE: *Stairs lead to a study above the main bedroom. The architects designed the plan with vistas through the entire house, which connect garden and lake.*

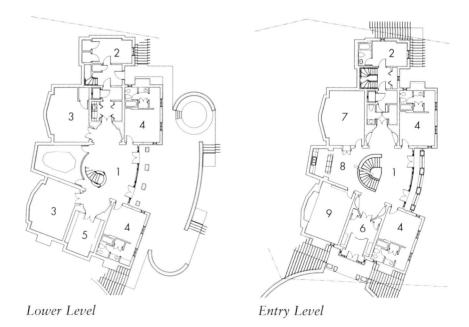

Lower Level   Entry Level

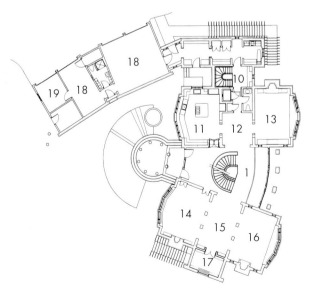

Upper Level

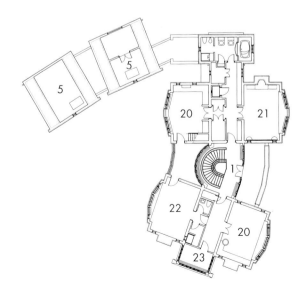

Top Level

1. HALL
2. STAFF QUARTERS
3. MECHANICAL
4. GUEST ROOM
5. STORAGE
6. ENTRY
7. THEATER
8. LOUNGE
9. GAME ROOM
10. OFFICE
11. KITCHEN
12. BREAKFAST ROOM
13. FAMILY ROOM
14. DINING ROOM
15. MUSIC HALL
16. LIVING ROOM
17. LIBRARY
18. GARAGE
19. WORKSHOP
20. STUDY
21. MAIN BEDROOM
22. TEA ROOM
23. READING ROOM

ABOVE AND RIGHT: *The central hall and balcony over it support Booth's assertion that "Each level has a different relation to the lake."*

PETER FORBES

HOUSE ON DEER ISLE, Maine, 1985

In the hands of architect Peter Forbes, the traditional New England forms of pitched roofs and stone chimneys become strong abstract sculpture. With its minimalist geometry and materials of lead-coated copper, glass, and cut stone, this seaside house is a modernist composition that simultaneously contrasts and blends with its spectacular site. Transparent walls dematerialize to allow tantalizing glimpses of water, heightening anticipation until the moment when the whole is revealed, or they materialize as mirrors to the surrounding birch and spruce forest. The glass is a foil for the stone of the chimneys, which visually anchor the house to the rock-ledged ground.

Forbes did not set out to design a house of separate elements. But consultations with the family revealed varying interests that made it logical to give parents, children, and guests individual quarters. The result is two glass pavilions: living-dining-kitchen spaces and the main bedroom, both for the parents. A third pavilion is for other family members. Once the whole was broken apart, the challenge became one of relating the parts. The architect angled the glass pavilions to open to one another, while the massive chimneys, like two great bookends, hold the composition together at the ends. "Without the stone chimneys," Forbes says, "the pavilions would be no more than transparent tents."

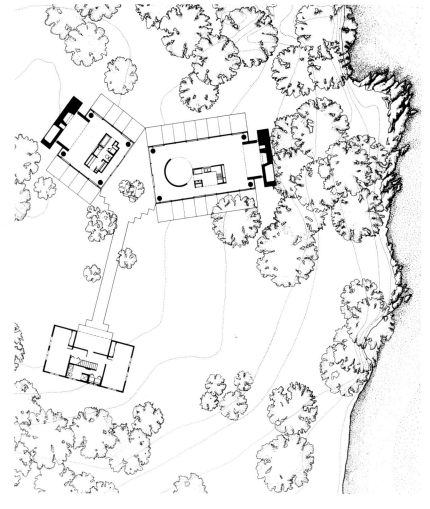

OPPOSITE AND PRECEDING PAGES: *The monolithic chimneys, built of native stone, ground the pavilions and fuse with the terrain. The almost freestanding stone masses engage the glass pavilions by penetrating under their roofs to form deep fireplaces.*

LEFT AND BELOW: *A serene inner wedge of manicured lawn and paving stones unites the buildings and also directs the gaze toward the ocean. Occupants are always aware of the other pavilions.*

OPPOSITE: *Outside the boundary of this cultivated clearing stands the rugged natural environment of forest, rocks, and ocean.*

ABOVE: *"The role of the architect," says Forbes, "is to edit among the spectrum of materials we have today." This corner shows the juxta-position of steel, concrete, and glass as well as stone. "Stone is precious. If it is used honestly with other materials," the architect says, "we recognize that each has a nobility."*

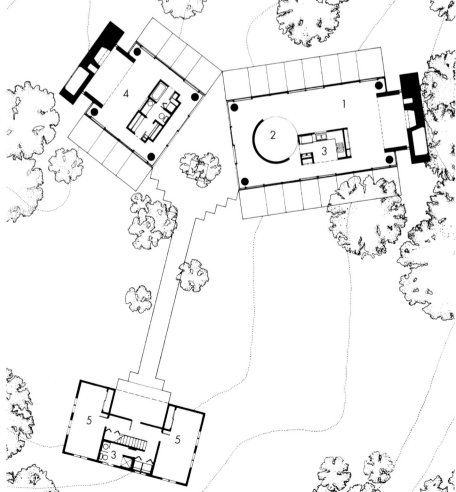

1. LIVING ROOM
2. DINING ROOM
3. KITCHEN
4. BEDROOM
5. GUEST ROOM

ABOVE: *The deep fireplace inglenook forms a separate room. "You need a refuge from the high ceilings and openness," says the architect. "The inglenook is enclosing, contrasting large and intimate scales. You also become aware of the colors and texture of stone when you're inside it."*

ABOVE AND RIGHT: *Four concrete piers define the corners of the pavilions and carry the weight of the tubular steel trusswork that supports the tentlike cedar ceiling planking, thus freeing the exterior walls for the great expanses of glass. The kitchen occupies its own "house" with a traditional window over the sink that frames a distant lighthouse island.*

OLSON SUNDBERG

HOUSE ON THE PRAIRIE, Highland Park, Illinois, 1991

The lines of this Highland Park house are strongly horizontal, stretching out to the surrounding prairie, long and low. The roofs float over stone walls that are solidly grounded, evoking the spirit of Frank Lloyd Wright. "When you work in Wright territory, you feel his presence," admits architect James Olson. "However, the ideas that developed in our design did so for the same reasons that they did in his work—to express a sense of the land." Wright was a hero of Olson's in school, but that does not mean that the architect does not introduce elements from other sources of inspiration. The spatial organization of the house, for example—symmetrical, with double axes—is classically formal. "More Palladian than Wrightian," says Olson.

The clients wanted a setting for their art collection, as well as a house that would focus on the beauty of a prairie nature preserve. The rear facade opens out to prairie bordered by a river, and indigenous plantings bring the prairie right up to the door. Olson and partner Richard Sundberg chose the Colorado sandstone of the walls for its earth-red tone, a color that gives more life to the greens of prairie grasses.

The interior spaces are both grounded and uplifting. A significant vista stretches from the entrance through the tall living room to the openness of the opposite wall and a dramatic view of prairie and river beyond. Windows drop below the floor and rise above the ceiling; the ceiling itself floats almost as if it is the sky, creating a sense of freedom. At the same time, limestone walls and stone floors counteract the weightlessness of the ceiling and the transparent wall. Olson, a modernist for whom the stone itself becomes the ornament, expresses his appreciation for the material: "It was a privilege," he concludes, "to use this much stone."

BELOW: *The design opens the house to nature on all sides. The southeast courtyard is full of flowers; its plantings shade the house from excessive sun.*

OPPOSITE: *The curving wall at the entrance provides privacy from the street and also serves as a metaphor for the separation between the cultivated world and the prairie wilderness embraced by the house. Horizontal sunscreens float airily above the stone walls.*

PRECEDING PAGES: *The marked horizontality of the major elements in the front facade recalls the many nearby houses of Frank Lloyd Wright.*

BELOW: *The sandstone enclosing the entrance gives a sense of compression that is in contrast to the openness and lightness of the living room.*
OPPOSITE: *A colonnaded gallery passes the major public spaces of the house and ends with a piece from the owners' art collection.*
OVERLEAF: *The richly colored limestone walls and stone floors anchor the living room, contrasting with the transparency of the glass window. Indirect lighting, pale plaster, and translucent*

panels of fabric surrounding the ceiling create the sense that the room expands both outward toward the prairie and upward toward the sky. "I call it exploding the box," says Olson. "It's an attempt to evolve the Prairie school into the next century."
SECOND OVERLEAF: *The most notable element of the rear facade of the house, which faces the prairie preserve and its river, is the overscaled glass wall of the living room, which glows like a lantern at night.*

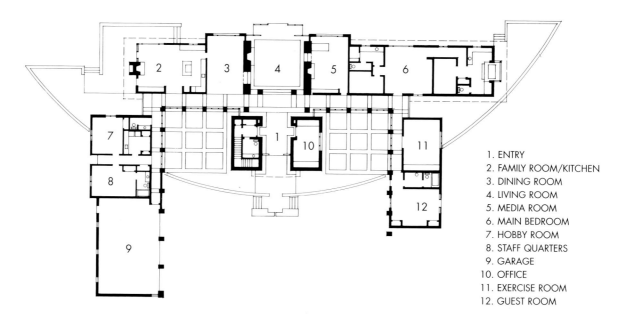

1. ENTRY
2. FAMILY ROOM/KITCHEN
3. DINING ROOM
4. LIVING ROOM
5. MEDIA ROOM
6. MAIN BEDROOM
7. HOBBY ROOM
8. STAFF QUARTERS
9. GARAGE
10. OFFICE
11. EXERCISE ROOM
12. GUEST ROOM

OLSON SUNDBERG

WRIGHT COTTAGE, San Juan Islands, Washington, 1994

The fieldstone of this vacation cottage is closely related to its rugged island setting in the San Juan chain near the Canadian border. The site is filled with dramatic outcroppings of lichen- and moss-covered rock that draw a visitor to sit, circle around, and meander through. The driveway curves past an enormous one, which serves as an introduction to the rough stone of the residence.

The original house was built in the 1920s of stones gathered on the property. When its restoration began, architect Anthony DeJesus of Olson Sundberg found that the stone walls could be preserved intact, which was important to the project. "The stone reflects the site," says DeJesus. Workers were able to demolish all of the interior framing for a new design. Changes included adding a loft over the kitchen, with a small dormer to admit additional light; enclosing the open porch to create a new entrance; and enlarging some windows. The house retains reminders of its past form through such various small irregularities as the outcroppings of stone left in front of a gabled door when it was converted from a window.

ABOVE: *A new entrance was created by enclosing an open porch.*

OPPOSITE: *Between the house and the shore is a meadow sloping down to a steep bluff. Below the meadow a crescent-shaped beach rims the quiet waters of the Strait of Juan de Fuca. Deer fencing encloses a garden to keep the island's considerable population from devouring flowers and vegetables. The small garden shed is a playhouse the owner bought at a charity auction.*

PRECEDING PAGES: *The restoration retained the original stone walls, so that from a distance, the cottage looks almost as if it has not changed since the 1920s.*

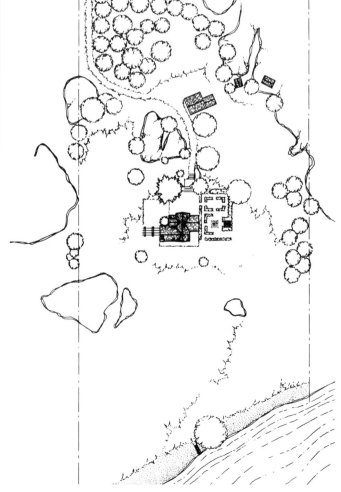

LEFT AND OPPOSITE: *The owner was closely involved in every detail of the project. Furnishings were kept simple and rustic. The two fireplaces are original, although the one in the dining room was refaced in concrete, a material more appropriate to the house than the original brick.*

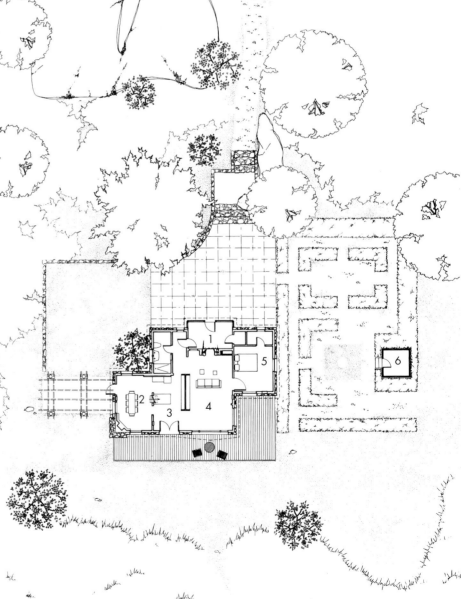

1. ENTRY
2. DINING ROOM
3. KITCHEN
4. LIVING ROOM
5. BEDROOM
6. GARDEN SHED

TAFT ARCHITECTS

TALBOT HOUSE, Nevis, West Indies, 1980

Both vernacular and British Colonial architecture influenced the design of this house on an island in the West Indies. The plan was conceived as four two-story structures of cut stone that define a central pavilion. While the design draws from the local tradition of adding buildings as a family grows, in organization the massing is formal, showing the influence of British colonization.

The spaces between the stone structures form four terraces. Thus each structure has exposures in all directions so that the oversized casement windows can catch the variable winds. The square windows help to develop proportional relationships by offering neither a horizontal nor a vertical reading. The spatial organization requires that the occupants pass into the communal pavilion before going to the rooms in the stone structures—three bedrooms and a kitchen.

The gray volcanic cut stone of the corner buildings was found on the site; it had probably been used in earlier structures there. To build most cost-effectively, partners John Casbarian, Danny Samuels, and Robert Timme designed the house to accommodate the contractor's previous experience. No construction drawings were necessary. Rainwater is collected by a system of gutters and pipes and stored in a thirty-five-thousand-gallon cistern below the central living pavilion; electricity is provided by kerosene. The exterior wood is painted in complementary red-orange and blue-green tones. Roofs on the island are either red or green, "colors that are felt to be neighborly," explains Casbarian.

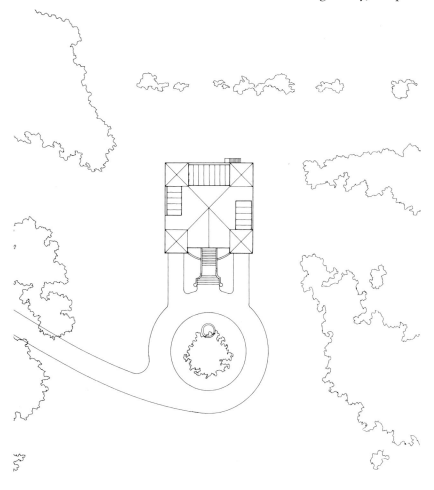

ABOVE: *The house is located halfway up Nevis Peak, overlooking the Caribbean. "We picked up on the way buildings were built in Nevis," says Casbarian. "A collection of smaller buildings makes a larger whole in response to the way the family grows."*
PRECEDING PAGES: *The symmetrical arrangement of corner structures, central pavilion, and terraces is immediately evident. Ground floors contain garages and workrooms.*

ABOVE: *A bedroom is visible from the entry terrace.*
RIGHT: *"We were very excited by the stenciling that local fishermen do on their boats," says Casbarian. Different floral friezes were hand-stenciled in each room; the rooms themselves are painted in pairs of complementary colors.*

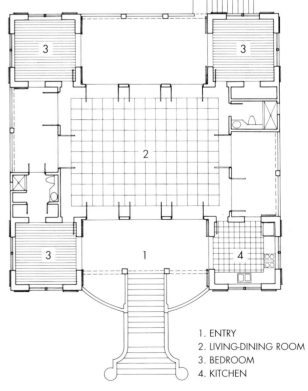

1. ENTRY
2. LIVING-DINING ROOM
3. BEDROOM
4. KITCHEN

MOUNTAINS

The secret of these hills was stone, and cottages
Of that stone made . . .
—STEPHEN SPENDER, "The Pylons"

BOHLIN CYWINSKI JACKSON

HOUSE IN THE ENDLESS MOUNTAINS, Northeastern Pennsylvania, 1995

The property, on a mountainside with views of a lake, horse pastures, an orchard, and distant mountains, was something of a no-man's-land; no obvious site for the house presented itself. To correct the problem, architect Peter Bohlin began with two significant design concepts. First, to achieve a sense of arrival, he created an automobile court, a rectangle defined by the proportions of the golden section and delineated by stone wall fragments, which resemble a ruin. Then he placed the principal living space on another "ruin," this one with a paving pattern recalling the foundation of a preexisting structure.

The actual foundation of the house, which extends outside, forms a level plinth—a flat lawn and terrace on the otherwise steep site. Bohlin observes that stone foundations found in the landscape have a mystery about them and a connection to the past: "In this case, we made a place with those qualities." A massive chimney, built of recycled stone from a demolished mill and reminiscent of the industrial architecture of the region, anchors the scheme. "The stone," says Bohlin, "was our way of rooting the building in that landscape and giving it a sense of place."

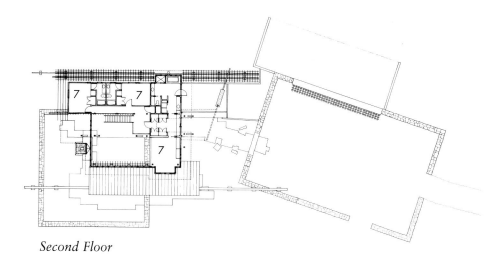

Second Floor

First Floor

1. ENTRY
2. STUDY
3. DINING ROOM
4. LIVING ROOM
5. KITCHEN
6. RETREAT
7. BEDROOM

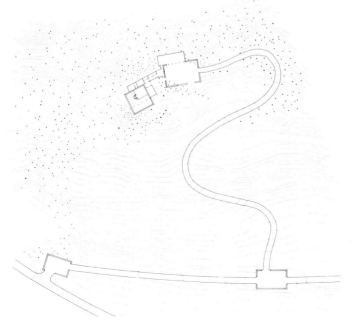

ABOVE: *Visitors pass through an auto court that creates a sense of arrival. Its partial walls appear to be a ruin. Indeed, many believe that the walls have always been there, something project manager Robert McLoughlin "takes as a compliment."*

PRECEDING PAGES: *The site slopes up into a forest behind the house; in front, the plinth raises the horizon, blocking out less desirable foreground views.*

RIGHT: *The path from the auto court to the main entrance, with its missing stones, continues the theme of the ruin.*

OPPOSITE: *The huge chimney is independent of the house, outside the glass walls and separate from the metal roof. The stone, graded from large at the bottom to small at the top, was retrieved from a demolished mill. Bohlin notes that some of the original mason's marks exist, "adding richness."*

ABOVE: *A stone bench passes through the glass at the main entrance. The vestibule is a single-height space that leads to the living room.*

LEFT: *The two-story, open-plan living room features a staircase and diagonal columns. Their bolts and straps are sculptural presences that break down the scale of the twenty-eight-foot-high space.*

OVERLEAF: *The fireplace and chimney both anchor the living room and give a sense of enclosure that contrasts with the transparency of the rest of the space. Beams, trusses, and the large firebox abutting the chimney suggest a human scale. Benches provide fireside seating, while radiant floor heat warms the room.*

BOHLIN CYWINSKI JACKSON

WEEKEND HOUSE, Maryland Mountains, 1995

The house is about the nature of stone and wood and how the two come together," says Peter Bohlin, designer of this sophisticated interpretation of a log cabin set on a rocky outcropping of forested mountainside. The architect employed the materials found in rustic buildings of the early twentieth century—stonework, logs, heavy timbers—reinterpreting them in ways that transcend the vernacular.

Rooms in the form of sheds are arranged loosely behind a massive U-shaped log wall, so that each room faces south, overlooking a valley. Within the area enclosed by the log wall, the architects created a quarrylike entry court, a landform of boulders and stone slabs that extends a ledge cut for an earlier cabin. The same stone becomes paving as it passes under the log wall; its ledges line the wall inside the house. The side of the house opposite the log wall is primarily of glass, offering a sunny vista.

The weightless transparency of the window wall contrasts with the solidity of the stone ledges and the log wall. Wood posts carry the roof; on the side with the stone ledges, they are footed on steel plates, suggesting the strength of the stone, whereas next to the glass wall, they punch through the wood floor to a structural system below, indicating the nonbearing capacity of the wood. Though the design is polished, Bohlin captured the rustic Adirondack camp character requested by the clients through his use of materials.

ABOVE: *The post-and-beam construction gives the illusion that the structure is growing out of the forest. "We made a natural element out of the stone and then the wood extends from the edge of the stone outward off the hillside," says Bohlin.*

OPPOSITE: *Wood columns support the sloped roof over the entry.*

PRECEDING PAGES: *The same stone ledges are visible both outside and inside the house. "The way in which the stone and wood come together makes the stone more poignant and the wood more touching as well," observes Bohlin.*

RIGHT: *The pool presents a "romantic vision of the landscape," says Bohlin, "with the land-form's rocky ledge, its hollow, and posts that are analogous to the forest."*

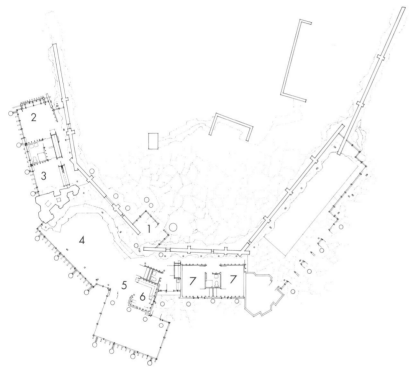

1. ENTRY
2. MAIN BEDROOM
3. STUDY
4. LIVING ROOM
5. DINING ROOM
6. KITCHEN
7. BEDROOM

ABOVE AND RIGHT: *Heavy timbers support the roof, freeing the exterior walls for glass. Clerestories are actually suspended from the roof and fit into slots on top of the walls. Ripple patterns in the stone indicate its original formation under water, "so you read the stone's past," observes Bohlin.*
OVERLEAF: *The wood columns supporting the house echo the trees on the mountainside.*

WILLIAM P. BRUDER

PLATT/LENTZ RESIDENCE, Maricopa County, Arizona, 1984

At dusk, when the interior is lit, the roof of this house seems to hover above the desert north of Phoenix like an object from outer space. Its spider frame and low pyramidal skylight appear to be suspended against the evening sky. On closer inspection, however, rugged stone and adobelike walls anchor the house firmly to the earth. Mediating between the walls and the roof are delicate trusswork and glass.

When David Platt, a master metalworker, asked Will Bruder to design the house, Platt specified that he would build it himself, a project that took forty-eight weekends. With a few helpers, he gathered stone for the walls—free tailings from the edges of nearby roads that had recently been graded—and packed them with a very dry mortar in two-foot-wide forms. (Frank Lloyd Wright used a similar method at Taliesin West.) Each weekend the builders lifted a completed segment into place atop the previous one. The segments are separated by 1/16-inch reveals that both create a taut resolution of the composition and serve as time markers celebrating a weekend's work. The walls, three feet thick, have a ten-inch thermal break for insulation; the insulation material is shredded computer printouts packed in cardboard lettuce boxes. The owner site-fabricated the roof of oil field drilling pipe that was weathered to a desert patina. It was lifted into place with a crane in only ten minutes. Bruder says of the house, "It's about the land, it's about minimalism, it's about sustainability, and yet there's a real earthiness about it."

The architect believes that when he listens well to a client, the first presentation of ideas honors the mission he's been asked to undertake. "They become owners," he says, "because they recognize themselves in those ideas. It's the discovery of the idiosyncratic nature of every client and their wants and passions and pragmatic needs that makes architecture special."

BELOW: *Bruder has been greatly influenced by ruins. "They represent ideas," he observes, "and architecture is as much about ideas as about physical realities." This house celebrates the idea of building a ruin. In the arid desert environment, the stone walls and steel truss roof will be standing centuries hence. "They'll form an interesting skeleton on the horizon, bonding with the massiveness of the earth and rising to meet the sky with the more delicate nature of the steel tube canopy," says the architect.*

OPPOSITE: *The front door is polished brass, copper, and glass. "The rocks tumbling out of the wall are sculptural rather than pragmatic," says Bruder, "a poetic gesture that bonds wall to land as the glass wraps around it."*

PRECEDING PAGES: *The horizontal stone-and-mortar segments that comprise the walls hug the desert, while the pyramidal skylight in the middle of the roof is a gesture toward the mountains.*

RIGHT: *The great room is a triangle, the geometrical basis for the plan of the house. Sculptural stainless-steel space conditioning ducts do not touch the ceiling; the room span thus remains open to dramatize the tension between the delicate-looking spider-frame roof and the three-foot thick masses of desert stone.*
OVERLEAF: *The evening sky emphasizes the drama inherent in Bruder's design.*

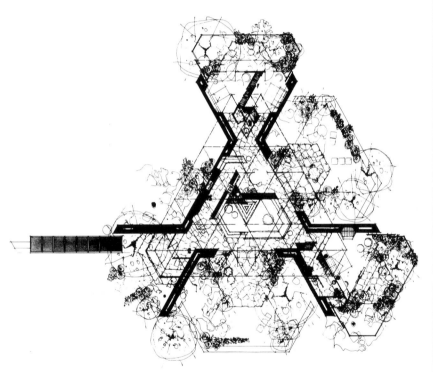

232   WILLIAM P. BRUDER

JONATHAN L. FOOTE

GUTHRIE RESIDENCE,
Jackson, Wyoming, 1992

The heavily wooded and secluded Snake River site has magnificent views of Grand Teton Mountain and the Cirques—two-to-three-thousand-foot cliffs that form great amphitheaters. Architect Jonathan Foote organized the house around selected views, choreographing the mountains by changing window proportions.

He describes the approach to the house as "a flow of space and events." A long, rustic road twists through cottonwoods, offering brief views of the mountainscape. It gives a sense of compression before opening to the climax of the trip, the house and a panorama of the vistas glimpsed only partially along the way.

The architect's design allows the husband and wife to live on just the upper floor when they are alone. The ground floor is devoted to the couple's teenage children and their activities. "Family closeness," says Foote, "is related to how well people can be separated." His plan provides privacy for all but does not neglect space for interacting.

PRECEDING PAGES: *Much of this area of Wyoming is without timber, while the river bottom furnishes a great deal of stone. For the dry-stack method of construction of this house, the mortar is set three or four inches back and the stones are tipped slightly forward for water runoff.*

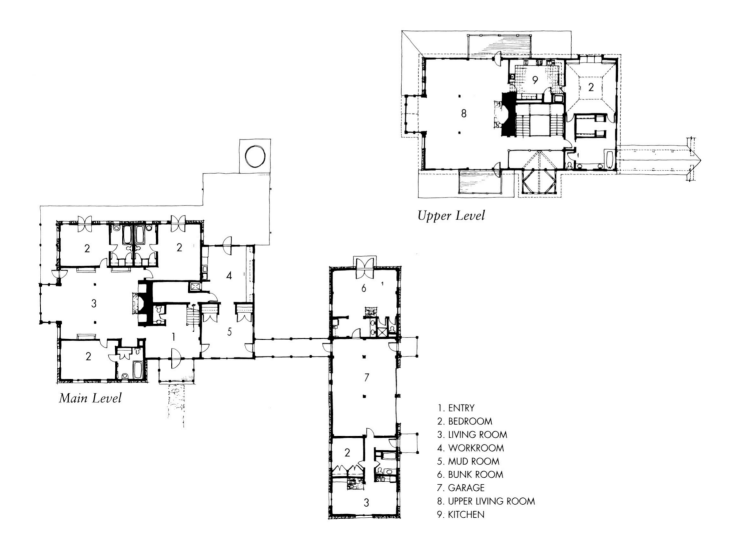

Upper Level

Main Level

1. ENTRY
2. BEDROOM
3. LIVING ROOM
4. WORKROOM
5. MUD ROOM
6. BUNK ROOM
7. GARAGE
8. UPPER LIVING ROOM
9. KITCHEN

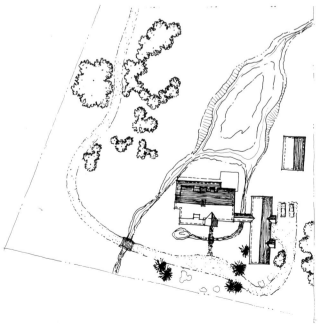

ABOVE: *In most of his houses, Foote creates a place he likes to call the "martini spot." Here it is located in front of the fireplace in the upper living room. Both Grand Teton and the Cirques are visible through different windows. The scale of the large living room was made more intimate by the rhythm of the exposed rafters. The decor reflects the clients' desire for the character of the West—but not the cowboy West.*

OVERLEAF: *The stone walls are eight inches thick and could easily carry the weight of the house, but code requirements demanded an alternative system—here, wood and steel framing—in case of earthquake.*

239

MARLYS HAHN

MOUNTAIN RETREAT, Catskill Mountains, 1985

A cruciform plan seemed an appropriate and harmonious design for this house, a weekend sanctuary for renewal. The site, on a rocky, forested mountainside overlooking a reservoir, was well suited for the purpose; architect Marlys Hahn found it imbued with spirituality. She created a one-room, open-plan design with four equal twenty-two-foot-high gable-roofed wings; the juxtaposed stone and glass impart the duality of the enclosing sense of a cave and the openness of a tree house.

Hahn chose the stones "for their energy and life." She purchased them from a neighboring farmer who was demolishing some fieldstone walls. In spite of the geometric forms, the subtle colors and texture of the stones, as well as the siting, blend the house into the existing rock ledges and the forest almost as though it were another natural element.

Traditional in its relationship to the landscape, the design is modernist in its influences. Hahn's inspirations for the spare plan were Mario Botta's symmetry and masonry, James Stirling's use of glass, and Louis Kahn's skill with light and silence. The house is open yet sheltering and elegant in its simplicity.

BELOW AND OPPOSITE: *Hahn believes that there should be no seams between inside and outside. Vast panes of glass draw the occupants into the landscape, while the stone provides a feeling of shelter. To reinforce the direct relationship between interior and exterior, floors are the same inside and out. The granite passes under the windows to pave the terraces.*
PREVIOUS PAGES: *The house is nestled into its site, with an extensive view down the mountain from the front and sheltering landforms at the rear.*

LEFT: *The glass-roofed kitchen-bath-storage wing faces the mountainside.*
OPPOSITE: *Expanses of glass in the other three wings create a direct link to the out-of-doors.*

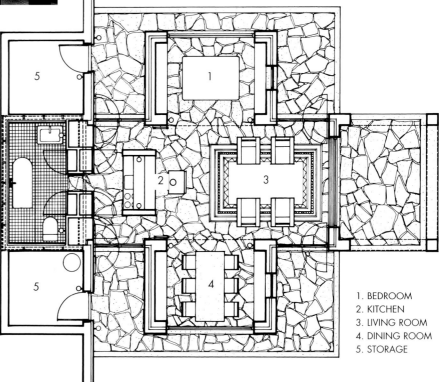

1. BEDROOM
2. KITCHEN
3. LIVING ROOM
4. DINING ROOM
5. STORAGE

ABOVE: *Because the four wings are extruded from the central space, snow fills the interstices in the winter, further merging the house and its site.*

RIGHT: *Even the narrow kitchen is connected to the exterior.*

OPPOSITE: *Sleeping lofts are located in the gables above the dining room and the ground-floor bedroom.*

ABOVE AND RIGHT: "*The feeling that you have the substance of a strong structure around you and the feeling that you can expand out into space are important foils to each other,*" *says Hahn.*

KOHN PEDERSEN FOX

CARWILL HOUSE, Stratton, Vermont, 1991

The site for this vacation retreat is a hillside with panoramic views of Stratton Mountain and the ski resort valley below. To maximize views and sunlight for the principal rooms, architect William Pedersen developed a collage of straight and curving planes and volumes that spin out pinwheel-like from a tall, central cylindrical volume at the entrance to the house. The design also minimizes the impact of the 5,600-square-foot volume on approach from the driveway. Pedersen had ten feet of bedrock cut away from the top of the hill to create an entry court between a sheer rock wall and the house, which is sited below the crest of the hill, thus framing the splendid mountain view.

Juxtaposed rectilinear and curvilinear volumes imbue the design with an abstract, minimalist quality. Yet the house draws on vernacular precedents. The layering of stone and wood and the pitched metal roofs refer to New England farmhouses. A system of horizontal cedar boards set an inch away from the weather enclosure of the house was inspired by the slatted sides of the humble corncrib, a form the architects found to have an appealing abstraction. Of the tall cylindrical form, senior designer Joshua Chaiken says, "We weren't necessarily thinking of a silo, but there it is."

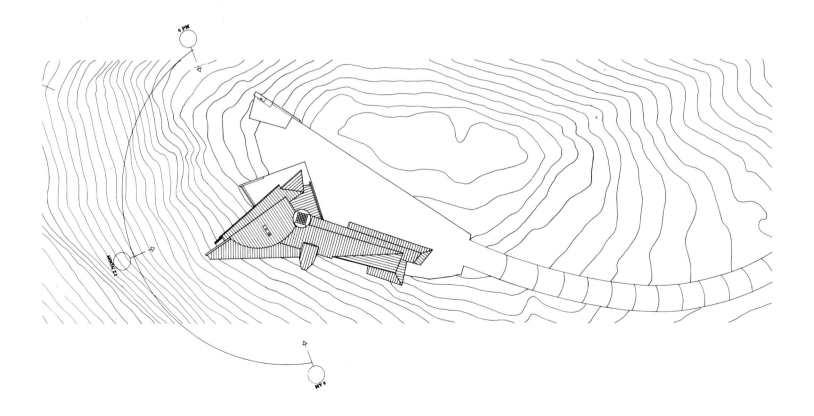

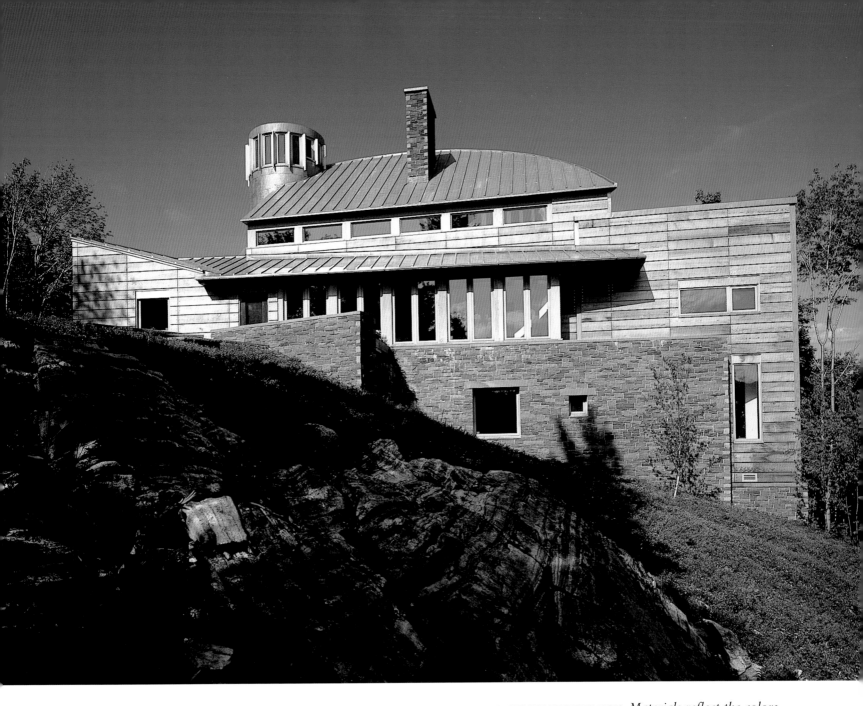

ABOVE AND PRECEDING PAGES: *Materials reflect the colors and textures of the mountain. In a layered sequence, the steeply pitched lead-coated copper roof meets walls of rough-surface cedar boards. Vermont slate, cladding the base walls and a large retaining wall, ties the house to the bedrock below the surface, evidenced by outcroppings on the hillside.*

LEFT AND OPPOSITE: *A hallmark of Pedersen's work is the dynamic juxtaposition of a taut curve and a straight line. Here the two create an arc that contains the living and dining rooms; a slate fireplace is poised between the two. The form of the ceiling is emphasized by clerestories on both the curved and flat wall surfaces.*

OVERLEAF: *The single-height kitchen opens to the double-height living room, which in turn closes to the single-height solarium. The solarium focuses the panoramic view.*

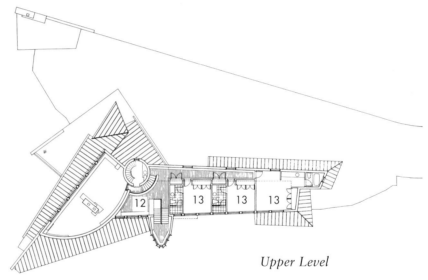

Upper Level

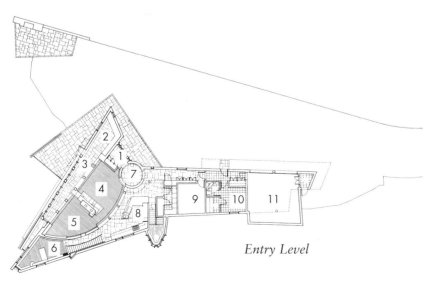

Entry Level

1. ENTRY
2. NORTH STUDY
3. SOLARIUM
4. LIVING ROOM
5. DINING ROOM
6. SOUTH STUDY
7. ROTUNDA
8. KITCHEN
9. MECHANICAL
10. BOOT ROOM
11. GARAGE
12. LOUNGE
13. BEDROOM

KEVIN ROCHE JOHN DINKELOO

NAPA VALLEY RESIDENCE, California, 1989

Early wineries in the Napa Valley were built of stone with heavy wood beams, as is this house. The vernacular precedent is particularly appropriate because the client's great-grandfather was a vineyard owner at the turn of the century. The courtyard around which the elements of the house are sited evokes a second vernacular influence—that of the region's Spanish missions.

Located on a small rise just off center in the valley, the house exploits both the height and the view. "As you enter the house, you look straight ahead, and on axis through the dining room you see Mount St. Helena," explains architect Kevin Roche. The house was inserted into the landscape without sacrificing any trees. In order to preserve the live oak in the courtyard and to maintain the axial view, especially careful siting of the house was required.

The mild climate allows a design impossible almost anywhere else, according to Roche. Stone walls—twenty inches thick with a moisture break but no insulation—are bearing. There are no screens; all doors disappear, permitting uninterrupted passage and views through the house from terrace on one side to vine-covered arcade and garden on the other. Interior stone walls merge with the exterior stone, further blurring the distinction between indoors and out. Other interior materials, such as wood beams and slate floors, provide a vocabulary of rustic simplicity.

FRANK VARGAS

ABOVE: *Wooden trellises step down to the pool and overlook the vineyards.*

OPPOSITE: *Entrance to the house is through the courtyard, a feature that draws on the historic missions of the region.*

PRECEDING PAGES: *Because it was placed on a small hill in the Napa Valley, the residence may be seen from a distance. It is in the midst of an oasis of trees, while the rest of the property is taken up with vineyards.*

ABOVE AND RIGHT: *All rooms open to the vine-covered arcade and courtyard garden; the stone walls and wood beams are repeated inside and out, binding the two. The pergola and its shadows, the stone columns, and the courtyard plantings create a visual richness.*

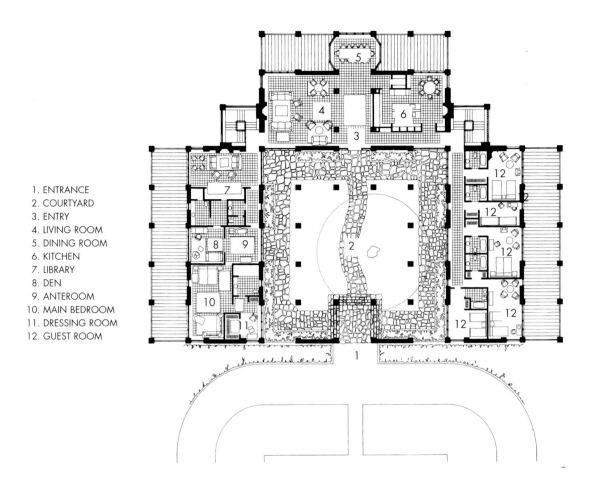

1. ENTRANCE
2. COURTYARD
3. ENTRY
4. LIVING ROOM
5. DINING ROOM
6. KITCHEN
7. LIBRARY
8. DEN
9. ANTEROOM
10. MAIN BEDROOM
11. DRESSING ROOM
12. GUEST ROOM

ABOVE, OPPOSITE, AND OVERLEAF: *Roche designed the low-key interiors using only natural materials—woven cottons and linens, wood and leather. No printed materials were used. All interior elements, such as the beams, were exposed wherever possible while still keeping the house "comfortable, friendly, and natural," says Roche.*

BIBLIOGRAPHY

BOOKS

Allport, Susan. *Sermons in Stone: The Stone Walls of New England and New York.* New York: W. W. Norton & Co., 1990.

Baker, John Milnes. *American House Styles: A Concise Guide.* New York: W. W. Norton & Co., 1994.

Bracken, Dorothy Kendall, and Maurine Whorton Redway. *Early Texas Homes.* Dallas: Southern Methodist University Press, 1956.

Carley, Rachel. *The Visual Dictionary of American Domestic Architecture.* New York: Henry Holt and Co., 1994.

Caro, Robert. *The Path to Power.* New York: Alfred A. Knopf, 1982.

Clark, Clifford Edward, Jr. *The American Family Home, 1800–1960.* Chapel Hill: University of North Carolina Press, 1986.

De Long, David G., Helen Searing, and Robert A. M. Stern, eds. *American Architecture: Innovation and Tradition.* New York: Rizzoli. 1986.

Farland, Mary Gray. *In the Shadow of the Blue Ridge.* Richmond: William Byrd Press, 1978.

Frasch, Robert W., Olaf William Shelgren Jr., Cary Lattin. *Cobblestone Landmarks of New York State.* Syracuse: Syracuse University Press, 1978.

Hewitt, Mark Alan. *The Architect and the American Country House, 1890–1940.* New Haven: Yale University Press, 1990.

Jordy, William H. *Progressive and Academic Ideals at the Turn of the Twentieth Century.* American Buildings and Their Architects, vol. 4. New York: Oxford University Press, 1972.

————. *The Impact of European Modernism in the Mid-Twentieth Century.* American Buildings and Their Architects, vol. 5. New York: Oxford University Press, 1972.

Keefe, Charles S., ed. *The American House, Being a Collection of Illustrations & Plans of the Best Country & Suburban Houses Built in the United States during the Last Few Years.* New York: U.P.C. Book Company, 1922.

Marshall, Howard Wight. *Paradise Valley, Nevada: The People and Buildings of an American Place.* Tucson: University of Arizona Press, 1995.

Massey, James C., and Shirley Maxwell. *House Styles in America.* New York: Penguin Studio, 1996.

McAlester, Virginia and Lee. *Great American Houses and Their Architectural Styles.* New York: Abbeville Press, 1994.

McGrew, Patrick, and Robert Julian. *Landmarks of Los Angeles.* New York: Harry N. Abrams, 1994.

McKee, Harley J. *Introduction to Early American Masonry: Stone, Brick, Mortar and Plaster.* Washington, D.C.: Preservation Press, National Trust for Historic Preservation, 1973.

Noble, Allen G. *Wood, Brick and Stone.* Amherst: University of Massachusetts Press, 1984.

O'Gorman, James F. *Three American Architects: Richardson, Sullivan, and Wright, 1865–1915.* Chicago: University of Chicago Press, 1991.

Patterson, Terry L. *Frank Lloyd Wright and the Meaning of Materials*. New York: Van Nostrand Reinhold, 1994.

Pearson, Clifford A., ed. *Modern American Houses: Four Decades of Award-Winning Design in Architectural Record*. New York: Harry N. Abrams, 1996.

Perrin, Richard W. E. *Historic Wisconsin Architecture*. Wisconsin Society of Architects of the American Institute of Architects, 1960.

Pierson, William H., Jr. *The Colonial and Neoclassical Styles*. American Buildings and Their Architects, vol. 1. New York: Oxford University Press, 1970.

———. *Technology and the Picturesque: The Corporate and the Early Gothic Styles*. American Buildings and Their Architects, vol. 2. New York: Oxford University Press, 1978.

Quiney, Anthony. *The Traditional Buildings of England*. London: Thames and Hudson, 1990.

Reynolds, Helen Wilkinson. *Dutch Houses in the Hudson Valley Before 1776*. Payson and Clarke for the Holland Society of New York, 1929; New York: Dover Publications, 1965.

Roth, Leland M. *A Concise History of American Architecture*. New York, Harper & Row, 1979.

Roth, Leland M., ed. *America Builds*. New York: Harper & Row, 1983.

Sanders, Scott R. *Stone Country*. Bloomington: Indiana University Press, 1985.

Schmidt, Carl F. *Cobblestone Masonry*. Scottsville, N.Y., 1966.

Scully, Vincent, Jr. *The Shingle Style and the Stick Style: Architectural Theory and Design from Downing to the Origins of Wright*. Rev. ed. New Haven: Yale University Press, 1971.

———. *The Shingle Style Today or the Historian's Revenge*. New York: George Braziller, 1974.

Stern, Robert A. M. *Architectural Monographs No. 17: Robert A. M. Stern, Selected Works*. New York: St. Martin's Press, 1991.

Upton, Dell, and John Michael Vlach, eds. *Common Places: Readings in American Vernacular Architecture*. Athens, Georgia: University of Georgia Press, 1986.

Welsh, John. *Modern House*. London: Phaidon Press, 1995.

Wilk, Christopher. *Marcel Breuer: Furniture and Interiors*. New York: Museum of Modern Art, 1981.

Williams, Henry Lionel, and Ottalie K. Williams. *A Guide to Old American Houses 1700–1900*. New York: A. S. Barnes and Co., 1962.

Winkler, E. M. *Stone in Architecture: Properties, Durability*. 3rd ed. Berlin: Springer-Verlag, 1994.

Wright, Frank Lloyd. *In the Cause of Architecture: Wright's Historic Essays for Architectural Record 1908–1952*. Edited by Hugh S. Donlan and Martin Filler. New York: McGraw-Hill, 1975, 1987.

Wright, Richardson, ed. *House & Garden's Second Book of Houses*. New York: Condé Nast Publications, 1925.

Zukowsky, John. *Hudson River Villas*. New York: Rizzoli, 1985.

ARTICLES

Bock, Gordon. "Stone Houses." *Old House Journal,* July-Aug. 1991, 26.

Breisch, Kenneth A. and David Moore. "The Norwegian Rock Houses of Bosque County, Texas: Some Observations on a Nineteenth-Century Vernacular Building Type." *Perspectives in Vernacular Architecture* 2 (1986): 64–70.

Friedberg, M. Paul. "Random Thoughts on Stone." *Building Stone Magazine,* Jan.-Feb. 1989, 11–15.

Giovannini, Joseph. "The Southland's Stone Age." *Los Angeles Conservancy News* 4, no. 1 (spring 1982): 1–4.

Hewitt, Mark Alan. "The Other Proper Style: Tudor Revival, 1880–1940." *Old House Journal,* Apr. 1997, 30–37.

Keister, Kim. "History Lesson: Samuel Chew's Cliveden." *Historic Preservation,* Nov.-Dec. 1993, 53.

Oxendorf, Eric. "Self-Portrait: Frank Lloyd Wright's Taliesin." *Historic Preservation,* Nov.-Dec. 1993, 29.

Sekowski, Katherine. "Thomas Balsley: In the Language of Natural Materials." *Building Stone Magazine,* July-Aug. 1992, 153–55.

Smith, C. W. "A Meditation on Stone." *Texas Architect,* July-Aug. 1995, 57–59.

Smith, Michael J. P. "Earth: Michigan Lithotecture." *Inland Architect,* May-June 1993, 97–98.

Touart, Paul B. "The Acculturation of German-American Building Practices of Davidson County, North Carolina." *Perspectives in Vernacular Architecture* 2 (1986): 72–80.

JOURNALS

Architecture
Architectural Digest
Architectural Record
Building Stone Magazine
Historic Preservation
Old House Journal